CHANDLER BEFORE MARLOWE

CHANDLER
BEFORE
MARLOWE

RAYMOND CHANDLER'S
EARLY PROSE AND POETRY,
1908-1912

EDITED BY MATTHEW J. BRUCCOLI
FOREWORD BY JACQUES BARZUN

UNIVERSITY OF SOUTH CAROLINA PRESS
COLUMBIA, SOUTH CAROLINA

Copyright © 1973 by the
UNIVERSITY OF SOUTH CAROLINA PRESS

Limited First Printing, July, 1973
Second Printing, July, 1973

Published in Columbia, S. C., by the
UNIVERSITY OF SOUTH CAROLINA PRESS, 1973

Manufactured in the United States of America

Library of Congress Cataloging in Publication Data

Chandler, Raymond, 1888–1959.
  Chandler before Marlowe.

  I. Title.
PS3505.H3224A6 1973   811'.5'2   72–13403
ISBN 0–87249–305–9

FOR ARLYN BARBARA BRUCCOLI

CONTENTS

ESSAYS AND SKETCHES: 1911-1912   53

REVIEWS: 1911-1912   83

THE YOUNG RAYMOND CHANDLER

JACQUES BARZUN

As an essayist, Chandler is known to the general public solely as the author of "The Simple Art of Murder." This sentimental piece glorifying the tough American tale and its hero has been much reprinted because it expresses a number of emotions that continue to haunt the insecure American mind: hostility to things English, resentment against both convention and corruption, and self-pity over the common lot, mixed with the illusion of self-reliance in the effort to down surrounding evils.

One of the interesting results of going back to Chandler's early essays and verse is to find the germs of these attitudes in a young writer who was not reared in America and who harbored them many years before the disillusionment of the Great Depression. But before one looks at these early records of feeling and opinion, it is only right to bear in mind one critical fact: whereas the "philosophy" of Philip Marlowe, the Galahad-detective, deserves only a smile when inspected in essay form, it is dramatically right for a hero in his situation, private and professional; and as such it is a splendid source of motive power in the great tales of Chandler's maturity.

Nor should the reader conclude that Chandler was nothing more than a story-teller. In the letters and other writings of his novelistic period that have been published and anthologized, he shows himself a better and sterner mind than in his war-horse essay on fictional murder. He is never an exact critic, but he often manages some detachment from his sense of wrong, and what he says suggests that he has read and reflected on literature at large, and not merely English and American detective fiction.

Now, thanks to the enterprise and devotion of Mr. Matthew Bruccoli, Chandler's admiring readers can round out their picture of the man and his mind, a mind that I think will seem in retrospect quite representative of the age. What is unusual about it is that its characteristic traits were in evidence well before Marlowe, before the Marxist Thirties, before the invention of Southern California as the natural theater of crime and concentrated vulgarity.

About Chandler's verses there is little to say except that they are without merit of any kind. The most searching detection does not discover one line capable of sticking in the memory, even when the author lifts whole phrases from Blake or Wordsworth. Only three pieces (one of them quite late and presumably inspired by the death of his wife) show any knowledge of contemporary diction and technique. What strikes us in the reading is the recurrent theme of being weighed down by some unnamed tyranny and the equally frequent defiance of it by the heroic ego. The poet calls upon Art or Thought or some other underdog entity to make war upon the resistless conspiracy of material interests. The verse, in short, contains in essence the root idea of all the later tales.

Now it is true that the primacy of art and beauty was a favorite theme of the Symbolist period in which Chandler came of age. But when he began to publish, the Nineties had *established* the superiority of art over commerce and politics and there was no reason, except in Chandler's inner self, for feeling put upon. That (as Marlowe might say) is the fishy bit that provides us with a clue.

Turn next to the essays, and observe that the first three, all in the last months of 1911, sound the note of angry dissent: "The Literary Fop," "The Genteel Artist," and "The Remarkable Hero" exhibit as many aspects of resentment tinged with envy, the target being the esthete. A literature of refinement is hateful to the young Chandler, and it is he who in connection with it raises the spectre of "the barricades." His later assumption that whatever is elegant is both sissyfied and corrupt underlies these short but effective diatribes, even though literature, not life, is their ostensible object.

For the positive side, we need only refer to "Realism and Fairyland," in which "life's refuse" (= realism) is embraced and equated with what is truly human, besides being representative of "a large class of people." Populism, realism, and moral egalitarianism are declared the premises of true art. By moral egalitarianism I mean the proposition that "We are all realists at times, just as we are all sensualists at times, all liars at times, and all cowards at times." This would be hard to prove, especially as to realism and sensuality, but as a political philosophy for novels of crime and corruption, it is perfect.

I do not want to spoil the reader's pleasure by going on and making a demonstration out of what should remain a suggestion, a quick look at the natural bent of Chandler's mind from his earliest days in literature. But two other small points are relevant and corroborative. One is the care and compression of the young man's prose. Chandler at 23 is in command of his means and enjoys putting things just so—even when he derides

xi

"the Phrasemaker." The other point is his insistence on one or two ideas, whether in verse or prose. That is unusual in so young a writer. The obsessive character of his thought, which gives the novels much of their power, is right here, full force, in these youthful pages, so happily gathered and restored to our inquisitive but sympathetic glance.

Columbia University

EDITOR'S PREFACE

MATTHEW J. BRUCCOLI

I found most of these "lost writings" while compiling *Raymond Chandler: A Checklist* (Kent, Ohio: Kent State University Press, 1968), and I have received conflicting advice about collecting them. The leave-them-buried group said that exhuming this material would be a disservice to Chandler, that he would have reprinted them himself if he had wanted them reprinted, and that this apprentice work isn't good or important. I am not really concerned with how good the material is, although I find it good—but not remarkably so—for the first published work of a writer in his early twenties. It is important and worth publishing only because it is Raymond Chandler's apprentice work. The conditions of this apprenticeship were special, for Chandler was not really an amateur. He started out as a professional: these pieces appeared in some of the best London journals, and he was paid for them. However, the apprenticeship led nowhere, for Chandler apprenticed himself to the wrong muse and the wrong master. The Raymond Chandler who wrote his first detective story, "Blackmailers Don't Shoot," in 1933 was the same man but a different writer. Twenty-one years in America provided him with material for his major work, and the writings of Ernest Hemingway, Dashiell Hammett, and the *Black Mask* school supplied models for his style and tone.

If Chandler had not written *The Big Sleep, Farewell, My Lovely, The High Window, The Little Sister, The Lady in the Lake, The Long Goodbye,* and *Playback,* this collection of his apprentice work would certainly not merit publication. The material simply does not stand up on its own. It reveals talent, but there is no flash of genius. Worse, it reveals a talent that is imitating poor models and refighting poetic battles. In short, Chandler fell into the traps set for young second-rate poets. He managed to combine self-pity and defiance; he has attitudes, but lacks his own material; he is in control of his emotions, but his emotions aren't strong. His writing is self-consciously literary and without a personal subject or power.

It comes down to this, then: If Raymond Chandler's novels are as good as some of us think they are, then all of his published work ought to be conveniently available for the sake of the light it sheds on his career.

❧ ❧

Raymond Chandler left Dulwich College in 1905 during his seventeenth year. Between 1908 and 1912—when he returned to America—he started a writing career that was not resumed until 1933 with publication of "Blackmailers Don't Shoot" in *Black Mask.*

Here is his account of that early period, taken from letters in

Raymond Chandler Speaking, edited by Dorothy Gardiner and Kathrine Sorley Walker (Boston: Houghton Mifflin, 1962):

When I was eighteen years old, my mother and my rich but dominating Irish uncle decided that I should take a Civil Service examination. . . . I wanted to be a writer, but I knew my Irish uncle would not stand for that, so I thought perhaps that the easy hours in the Civil Service might let me do that on the side. I passed third in a group of about six hundred. I went to the Admiralty, but found the atmosphere so stultifying that after six months I resigned. This was a bombshell; perhaps no one had ever done it before. My Irish uncle was livid with rage. So I holed up in Bloomsbury, lived on next to nothing, and wrote for a highbrow weekly review [The Academy] and also for The Westminster Gazette, perhaps the best evening paper the world ever saw. But at the best I made only a very bare living.
. . . J. A. Spender was the first editor who ever showed me any kindness. He was editing The Westminster Gazette in the days when I worked for him. I got an introduction to him from a wonderful old boy named Roland Ponsonby Blennerhasset, a barrister with a House of Lords practice, a wealthy Irish landowner (he owned some fabulous number of acres in Kerry), a member, as I understood from my uncle in Waterford, of one of these very ancient untitled families that often make earls and marquesses appear quite parvenu. Spender bought a lot of stuff from me, verses, sketches, and unsigned things such as paragraphs lifted from foreign publications. He got me into the National Liberal Club for the run of the reading-room. I was seconded by his political cartoonist, a famous man in those days, but I have forgotten his name. I never met him in the flesh.
I got about three guineas a week out of all these, but it wasn't enough. I also worked for a man named Cowper [i.e., Cecil Cowper, J. P., editor of The Academy, 1910–1916] who succeeded Lord Alfred Douglas in ownership of The Academy, and did a lot of book reviewing for him, and some essays which I still have, they are of an intolerable preciousness of style, but already quite nasty in tone. I seldom got the best books to review, and in fact the only one of any importance I got my hands on was The Broad Highway (Jeffrey Farnol) for whose author,

then unknown, I am glad to say I predicted an enormous popularity. I reviewed Eleanor Glyn and how. Like all young nincompoops I found it very easy to be clever and snotty, very hard to praise without being ingenuous.

. . . I wrote quite a lot of verses for *The Westminster Gazette* also, most of which now seem to me as deplorable, but not all, and a good many sketches, mostly of a satirical nature—the sort of thing Saki did so infinitely better. As a matter of fact, I had only the most limited personal contact with Spender. I would send the stuff in, and they would either send it back or send me proof. I never corrected the proof, I simply took it as a convenient form of acceptance. I appeared regularly on a certain day each week at their cashier's office and received payment in gold and silver, being required to affix a penny stamp in a large book and sign my name across it by way of receipt. What a strange world it seems now!

I suppose I have told you of the time I wrote to Sir George Newnes and offered to buy a piece of his trashy but successful weekly magazine *Tit-Bits?* I was received most courteously by a secretary, definitely public school, who regretted that the publication was not in need of capital, but said that my approach had at least the merit of originality. By the same device I did actually make a connection with *The Academy*. . . . (Cowper) was not disposed to sell an interest in his magazine, but pointed to a large shelf of books in his office and said they were review copies and would I care to take a few home to review. I wonder why he did not have me thrown down his murky stairs; perhaps because there was no one in the office who could do it since his entire editorial staff seemed to consist of one placid middle-aged lady and a mousy little man named Vizetelly. . . .

I met there also a tall, bearded, and sad-eyed man called Richard Middleton, of whom I think you may have heard. Shortly afterwards he committed suicide in Antwerp, a suicide of despair, I should say. The incident made a great impression on me, because Middleton struck me as having far more talent than I was ever likely to possess; and if he couldn't make a go of it, it wasn't very likely that I could. Of course in those days as now there were popular and successful writers, and there were clever young men who made a decent living as free lances for the numerous literary weeklies and in the more literary departments of the daily papers. But most of the people who did this work either had private incomes or jobs, especially in the civil service. And I was distinctly not a clever young man. Nor was I at all a happy young man. I had very little money, although there was a great deal of it in my family.

◅℥ ℥▻

I have not located all of Chandler's apprentice work; the unsigned paragraphs he contributed to the *Westminster Gazette* are apparently unidentifiable.

Two poems, "Requiem" and "Sonnet 13," depart from the scope of this collection. "Requiem" was written after Chandler's wife, Cissy, died in 1954; it was accepted by the *Atlantic Monthly* in 1957 but never published. I have included it because it is too good to waste. The working draft of "Sonnet 13" was facsimiled in *Tutto Marlowe Investigatore*, I (Mondadori, 1970) and has been reprinted here to make it more available in America.

The unsigned reviews in this collection are attributed to Raymond Chandler on the basis of clippings in the possession of Helga Greene, executrix of his estate. It is therefore evident that I owe a great debt to Mrs. Greene. I also thank Kathrine Sorley Walker, Jennifer E. Atkinson, Charles Mann, I. S. Skelton, and the superb staff of The British Museum.

University of South Carolina

CHANDLER BEFORE

VERSE:
1908-1912

MARLOWE

Chambers's Journal, XII (19 December 1908), 48.

The Unknown Love.[1]

When the evening sun is slanting,
When the crickets raise their chanting,
And the dewdrops lie a-twinkling on the grass,
As I climb the pathway slowly,
With a mien half proud, half lowly,
O'er the ground your feet have trod I gently pass.

Round the empty house I wander,
Where the ivy now is fonder
Of your memory than those long gone away;
And I feel a sweet affection
For the plant that lends protection
To the window whence you looked on me that day.

Was it love or recognition,
When you stormed my weak position
And made prisoner my heart for evermore?
For I felt I long had known you,
That I'd knelt before the throne you
Graced in Pharaoh's days or centuries before.

Though your face from me was hidden,
Yet the balm was not forbidden
On your coffin just to see the wreath I sent.
Though no word had passed between us,
Yet I felt that God had seen us
And had joined your heart to mine e'en as you went.

Let them talk of love and marriage,
Honeymoon and bridal carriage,

And the glitter of a wedding *à la mode!*
   Could they understand the union
   Of two hearts in dear communion
Who were strangers in the world of flesh and blood?

   In my eyes the tears are welling
   As I stand before your dwelling,
In my pilgrimage to where you lived, my fair.
   And ere I return to duty
   In this world of weary beauty,
To the stillness of the night I breathe my prayer:

   When the last great trump has sounded,
   When life's barque the point has rounded,
When the wheel of human progress is at rest,
   My belovèd, may I meet you,
   With a lover's kiss to greet you,
Where you wait me in the gardens of the blest!

R. T. CHANDLER.

4

The Westminster Gazette, XXXIII (3 March 1909), 2.

The Poet's Knowledge.

There is no thought born in man's brain
    Which I too have not known;
There is no single joy or pain
    I have not made my own.

Beside the grimmest tragedy
    A witness I must stand.
Long buried griefs are near to me
    As my ink-spattered hand.

O maiden weeping all alone
    For your unfaithful love,
Think not your sorrow only known
    To Him who reigns above!

O mother mourning for your child,
    With cheeks of pallid hue,
Long after you have once more smiled
    My tears pour down for you.

O tyrant with the sneering face,
    O victim 'neath the knife,
O saint sublime and sinner base,
    I too have lived your life.

O thinker groping in the gloom,
    Torn by a nameless fear,
You think your anguished shriek of doom
    Unuttered, yet I hear.

I stand behind the judgment seat,
  I plunge across hell's brink.
And all to place upon a sheet
  A line of fading ink.

R. T. Chandler.

The Westminster Gazette, XXXIII (5 March 1909), 2.

The Soul's Defiance.

It matters not what strife has riven,
    What hydra-headed tyrants reign,
Man can but take what man has given,
    A drop of blood, an ounce of gain.

What though some monster's bloodstained
    foot
    Crush me in his chaotic race?
Stamp out my being to the root?—
    I laugh into his frenzied face.

I fear no juggernaut of wrath
    Propelled by man's fanatic rage.
I stand undaunted in its path,
    The champion of a wiser age.

The tyrants cry: "A scoffer killed!"
    And write me on their victims' roll.
They think my voice forever stilled,
    Poor fools! they have but freed my
    soul!

I fear not where that soul may go,
    It matters not what gods there be,
They did enough their might to show
    Had they done naught but fashion me!

                R. T. CHANDLER.

The Westminster Gazette, XXXIII (26 March 1909), 2.

The Wheel.

The world expends its useless might,
The heaving nations toil and fight,
The dizzy thinker peers for light,
The day doth follow day and night,
    Is there no rest from anything?

The lover gives another heart,
The merchant finds another mart,
The young men have their lives to start,
The old reluctantly depart,
    Is there no rest from anything?

The gloomy sigh that life is pain,
The buoyant call each day a gain,
The doubter cries that nought is plain,
The cynic sneers that hope is vain,
    Is there no rest from anything?

The worshippers their gods appease,
The tortured sinner moans for ease,
The speed of things doth not decrease,
The Wheel of Things doth never cease,
    Is there no rest from anything?

What is the end of toil and thought?
What is the jewel we have sought?
What is the work that we have wrought?
Can nothingness end but in nought?
    Can there be rest from anything?

"Fool! rest shall come when stones can feel,
Fool! rest shall come when poisons heal,
Fool! rest comes not at thy appeal,
Fool! thou art bound upon the Wheel,
   There is no rest from anything!"

R. T. CHANDLER.

The Westminster Gazette, XXXIII (16 April 1909), 2.

Art.

When the first man laid the thicket
  low,
And hewed the virgin tree,
He had no thought that every blow
Prepared the way for Me.

When the hunter fought the mastodon
With flint-axe swinging free,
He had no thought that, lost or won,
The issue was to Me.

When the pioneer defied the waste
And crept from sea to sea,
Knew he that every hardship faced
Was faced to honour Me?

When the soldier lead a mighty host
To a mighty victory,
Knew he that glory and its cost
Were gained and paid for Me?

When the politician reared a state
And filled a history,
The fame he made endureth late,
But it belongs to Me.

When the merchant toiled in his
  counting-house,
When the lawyer made his plea,
They did but as the sheep that browse,
And did it all for Me.

For all men did, and all men do,
And all that done shall be,
Is but a paltry grain or two
Of incense burned to Me.

Ye think ye worship gods for hope
Of all eternity,
But all are bound on a single rope,
And the rope is held by Me.

And if ye serve the blazing sun,
Or a god ye cannot see,
And if your gods are ten or one,
Ye only worship Me.

Ye may despise my name and face,
Deride my mastery;
Another task in another place
Ye do—and do for Me.

For ye that blame and ye that praise
Are vassals in my fee,
And ye may go a million ways,
But all ways lead to Me.

'Tis little that I let ye know
Of truth and mystery,
But never while the aeons flow
Shall ye know aught but Me.

I am the thinker and the thought,
The workman and the task;
I am the lesson I have taught,
The question that I ask.

I am the ruler and the law,
The victim and the knife;
I am the vessel and the flaw,
The fighter and the strife.

I am the villain and his curse,
The martyr and his stake;
I am the poet and his verse,
The steamer and its wake.

I am the doubt which clouds your
    mind,
The mind which feels the doubt;
I am the branches and the wind,
The vanquished and the rout.

I am the lover and his kiss,
The seeker and his find,
The Is and Was, the That and This,
The kernel and the rind.

And ye must do what I ordain,
Although ye know it not,
And if 'tis joy, and if 'tis pain,
Remembered or forgot.

The future, present, and the past,
Are hairs upon my hand;
The heaven I give ye at the last
Is but to understand.

   R. T. CHANDLER.

The Westminster Gazette, XXXIII (22 April 1909), 2.

A Woman's Way.

Come with me, love,
     Across the world,
Ere glory fades
     And wings are furled,
And we will wander hand in hand,
Like a boy and girl in a playroom land.

Stay with me, love,
     In the city's murk,
Where the sun but dares
     Shyly to lurk,
And we will watch life hand in hand,
Like a boy and girl in a grown-up land.

Go from me, love,
     If thou 'lt not stay;
Follow thy bent,
     'Tis the better way.
And I will seem to hold thy hand,
Like a child in dreams of fairyland.

I must leave thee, love?
     'Tis I must go?
Then as thou wilt,
     For thou must know.
Let me but think I hold thy hand,
I'll roam content in any land.

R. T. CHANDLER.

The Westminster Gazette, XXXIII (2 June 1909), 2.

The Quest.

I sought among the trampling herds of men
   That choke the cities of the east and west.
The proudest mansion and the foulest den
   I entered, seeking wisdom yet unguessed.
I searched them through unpausing, without rest,
   Until the bricks and plaster of each wall
Became transparent at my thought's behest,
   But still I could not hear the Master's call.

I wandered on the moorland and the fen,
   I climbed the mountain to its silent crest,
I watched the robin redbreast and the wren
   Choose out the leaves wherewith to build a nest.
I looked upon the plain by dawn caressed,
   I saw its contours gaunt beneath night's pall.
All nature told her tale at my behest,
   But still I could not hear the Master's call.

I thought to keep all knowledge in a pen,
   All human hardship was to me a test,
There seemed naught undiscovered to my ken,
   But that I sought I found nowhere expressed.
I left my learning for a maiden's breast,
   I scorned my wisdom to become her thrall,
Blasphemed my task at her unspoke behest,
   But still I could not hear the Master's call.

She spurned the love which all my soul possessed,
  She threw it down and jested at its fall.
I laughed and turned to recommence my quest,
  And in the laugh I heard the Master's call.

                    R. T. CHANDLER.

The Westminster Gazette, XXXIII (9 June 1909), 2.

When I Was King.

I see it in the smoke-land
    After my daily bout
With the hard, old world of reason,—
    I see my splendid rout,
The time I trod Valhalla
    And chose my goddess out.

Yet 'twas not I who chose her,
    A spirit took my part,
Lit up my vagrant fancies
    With a gleam of heaven's art,
Led on my lost battalions,
    Cheered on my coward heart.

It was a thing of glory,
    The temple that I wrought,
Though ev'ry column in it
    With living hope was bought,—
A temple fit for Juno,
    As even Juno thought.

She saw me as a Viking,
    With strength no Viking had;
She saw me as a Bayard,
    The sane among the mad.
She deemed it brave to fear me,
    My coldness made her glad.

Scarce would she let me love her
    Lest I forgo my crown,
And be no more a hero

16

To bend men with a frown.
(Methinks I was a hero
  Who threw a hero down!)

So bit by bit I showed her
  The wonders of the shrine,
The temple of my manhood
  I reared to charm her eyne.
And then—ah, had I faltered
  Nor blotted the design!

But no. Behind the altar
  I pointed to a door,
And opened it, and waited,
  Erect and calm as Thor.
Her worship fell to scorning,
  And lifted nevermore.

Ev'n then, if I had grovelled,
  Condemning my deceit,
Her white, majestic bosom
  Mayhap to mine had beat.
But a fire of strength burned in me
  With more than human heat.

For I am weak as water,
  The might I made her see
Was breath of some far power
  That willed to make me free,
A moment's king of heaven,
  Too tall for one low plea.

'Tis gone, my painted temple,
  Elysium of fraud;
But she, in her despising
  Some other vessel flawed,
May think of my Valhalla
  And me, her broken god.

R. T. Chandler.

The Westminster Gazette, XXXIII (18 June 1909), 2.

The Hour of Chaos.

It cometh at the height of thy attaining,
It cometh in the pit of thy profaning,
Or in the noonday of thy noble straining,
Or in the twilight of thy purpose waning,
    The time when thou must lose the way of things.

Then findest thou no guide in lettered pages,
No beacon in the flame of fleshly rages,
No shelter in the bars of gilded cages,
But thou must doubt of all thy work and wages
    Alone in all the blinding day of things.

Then doth thy rock of trusting cleave asunder,
Then do thy garnered sheaves appear as plunder
Torn from a weaker vessel crushed under,
A finer spirit deafened by the thunder
    And endless roaring of the storm of things.

Then all the powers with their sceptres gleaming,
And all the graces erstwhile pure and beaming
Become the nightmare spectres of thy dreaming
And all the world is a disordered teeming
    And angry writhing of the worm of things.

Then love and glory flowering for ever
Are barren as the desert blooming never,
And mighty life is but a useless lever
To raise and join what mighty death shall sever,
    And nature is the simple fool of things.

Then men are like a frenzied herd of bison,
And all creation is a vasty prison,
And night no blacker than when day hath risen
A mocking torch to light the sear and wizen,
  And God Himself is but the tool of things.

R. T. CHANDLER.

The Westminster Gazette, XXXIII (29 June 1909), 2.

The Bed of Roses.

The world is a bed of roses,
    The roots are sunk in hell,
The blossoms rear to heaven,
    The thorns are long and fell.

A yokel comes with a sickle
    And hews with heavy scorn,
And reaps a mingled harvest
    Of petal, stalk, and thorn.

But a poet wails unnoticed
    Anear the trampled bed,
And waters it and watches
    Till a rose-bud lifts its head.

And then he plucks it quickly,
    And quickly steals away,
For the yokel cometh lusty
    For another harvest day.

The poet showeth no man
    The rose-bud next his heart,
But praiseth it in story,
    And the story men call art.

                R. T. CHANDLER.

The Westminster Gazette, XXXIV (29 July 1909), 2.

The Reformer.

An Eastern king sat on his throne
  To judge a fettered slave,
For he had come in the night alone
  To send the king to his grave.

The king leaned back with a weary air,
  And tapped the ground with his foot.
The slave was bound with his own long
    hair,
  Torn from his head by the root.

"My captains slept in easy call,
  Two guards stood by my door;
My hound that heareth each footfall
  Lay by my bed on the floor.

"And yet thou camest in the night
  Unheard as a thread of smoke,
And as thy knife was up to smite
  I started and awoke.

"A moment long into thy face
  I looked and made no cry.
Now tell me why thou gavest grace
  And let thy chance go by."

The slave threw back his bleeding head
  And smiled a scornful smile.
"Dread is thy name, O King," he said,
  "For a tyrant dark and vile.

"I held to slay thee in the night
 At my life's cost were cheap,
Yet do not murder for delight
 Nor slay men in their sleep.

"And when thou didst awake, O King,
 I looked deep in thine eye,
And saw no fear nor faltering,
 So let my chance go by.

"For though thou hast an evil name
 Thou hadst an evil school,
And I had earned as ill a fame
 To slay so brave a fool."

The king showed all his gleaming teeth
 In a laugh full loud with glee,
Then quickly seized his jewelled sheath
 And flung his right arm free.

"Now cast me off his bonds," he cried,
 "And give him back his knife.
My sword and Allah shall decide
 If he shall keep his life."

The captains ranged about the throne
 Murmured with grim surprise.
A white-haired chief stepped forth alone
 And met his master's eyes.

"It is not meet my King and Lord
 Do battle with a slave.
It is not meet a noble sword
 Should carve so foul a grave."

Louder the king spoke his command,
 None moved to do his hest.
The aged chief plucked out his brand
 And pierced the bound slave's breast.

"*The stain is mine, my King and Lord.*"
    The old chief bent his head,
Then shortened his polluted sword,
    Struck inwards, and fell dead.

The king stood o'er the bodies twain
    And gazed deep and long.
Then loud and clear he laughed again
    And passed out from the throng.

At sunset when the muezzins call
    The faithful unto pray'r,
They sought the king in court and hall
    But no man found him there.

     .   .   .   .

Another king reigns in that land,
    A wiser king is he;
Four guards without his chamber stand,
    Within his hounds are three.

           R. T. CHANDLER.

The Westminster Gazette, XXXIV (30 September 1909), 2.

The Perfect Knight.

He hath a sword of altar fire,
    He hath a shield of shimmering air,
The one to slay his base desire,
    The one to guard him from despair.

He hath a burnished helm of laughter,
    He hath a lance of righteous wrath,
To gild the smoke-stain on his rafter,
    To dash the foul thing from his path.

He hath a gauntlet of emotion,
    He hath a prancing steed of love,
He hath a banner of devotion
    To lead wherever he may rove.

He hath a mind to see and wonder,
    A soul to answer to his sight,
A heart of song and mighty thunder,
    A voice of endless pure delight.

He hath a vast and sunny garden
    To tend through unexhausted time,
With Israfil to be its warden,
    With flowers meet for every clime.

His strength is higher than the mountain,
    And older than the universe,
Why doth he thirst beside his fountain
    And seek for nothing with a curse?

E'en in his fury is he craven,
   Glaring he wails he cannot see;
He hides his head and prays for Heaven,
   Who hath all Heaven in his fee.

R. T. CHANDLER.

The Westminster Gazette, XXXIV (8 November 1909), 2.

A Pilgrim in Meditation.

My heart hath brooded in the world of shadow,
And it hath sported in the world of sunlight,
And drooped with languor in the world of dreaming,
And hotly striven in the world of waking,
And gathered rapture in the world of gladness,
And sunk with grieving in the world of sorrow.

But through the tangled spectre-land of shadow,
I saw the distant flashing of the sunlight,
And through the heavy sweetness of my dreaming
I felt the iron vigour of my waking,
And fought with sorrow in the lists of gladness,
And clung to joyance in the pool of sorrow.

And never could I find a path of shadow
That did not wander o'er a hill of sunlight,
And never could I fill my sense with dreaming
But ere the hunger died there came a waking,
And never could I carve a form of gladness
But it was flawed by some dark knot of sorrow.

Wherefore there was no meaning in the shadow
Save as the dusky fellow of the sunlight;
There was no plenty in the hoard of dreaming
Save it was stolen from the wealth of waking;
There was no ripple in the stream of gladness
But answered to a hidden weed of sorrow.

Wherefore I know hell is not built of shadow
Nor heaven the abode of fadeless sunlight,
Nor all is madness in the land of dreaming,

Nor all is noble in the land of waking,
And there were torture in the halls of gladness
Unborne without the numbing touch of sorrow.

So is he lame who ever walks in shadow,
And he is blind who ever peers in sunlight,
And he is dead who lives alone for dreaming,
And soulless he who knoweth only waking,
A demon's jest who knoweth only gladness,
A demon's groan who knoweth only sorrow.

R. T. CHANDLER.

The Westminster Gazette, XXXIV (17 November 1909), 2.

The Pioneer.

I sang a song of glory.
　　They said it will never die;
But the beauty charmed to the singing
　　With the end hath passed me by.
For I think my own heart told it
　　Were heaven in the nook
Where I sang the song of glory,
　　I would not turn to look.

I sang a song of a maiden,
　　Beautiful, wronged, divine;
It dimmed their eyes with weeping,
　　It cannot moisten mine.
A love lay on my spirit,
　　I owned and held it fast
When I sang the song of a maiden,
　　But now the song is past.

I sang a song of a hero,
　　The hot blood surged to the cheek,
And made the hearers wonder
　　That a man could e'er be weak.
A mighty joy was in me,
　　Untainted, calm, and sure;
But the song is sung, and after
　　The joy could not endure.

So each note as I loosed it
　　Swiftly went out from me

To the hearts of them that listened,
  To hearts as yet to be.
I know they raised the fallen,
  And softened many a groan;
I know they made men fellows,
  But me they left alone.

The reaper joys in the harvest
  Long after the winter comes;
The soldier dreams of his battles
  Beside the broken drums;
But the poet climbs to the future,
  His song is a journey-staff,
His voice may sweeten oceans,
  But he may not pause to quaff.

They that are done their labour
  Take down a treasured tome,
And drink in strength and beauty
  In the quiet of their home.
But the poet, tense and eager,
  Is mounting the peak of time,
And peering across the darkness
  For a higher, purer clime.

Though his gold have filled the cities
  In never-thinning store,
He seeketh a rarer metal,
  An undiscovered ore.
Though sky and earth and ocean
  With the ancient echoes ring,
The poet only listens
  For the songs that are yet to sing.

R. T. CHANDLER.

The Westminster Gazette, XXXV (28 February 1910), 2.

The Hermit.

As with a low-bent head and empty gaze
I pace along the temple of still gloom,
And wonder if my feet have left the ways
Of life, and passed unknowing to the tomb,
My garment whispers to the stones of death,
And from the darkness and the pillared shade
There stirs a shape of half-embodied breath
That stalks as it would make my heart afraid.
It is the friend I chose me in the past,
Shaking the dust of mankind from my robe,
And side by side we wander at this last
Into the night we care no more to probe:
    He the pale image of my scorning wrought,
    And I that slew the world with my own thought.

R. T. CHANDLER.

The Academy, 14 May 1910, p. 462.

The Dancer

She with her own sad mystery of grace
Steals through our senses like a wailing air
Steals through the moonlight, she is strangely fair
And magical with beauty; none shall trace
Her lips of braided flame or her sweet face
Of frozen wind, and none arise to share
The dark and sweet disaster of her hair;
There is but one such star in all the space!

Our hearts are as a garden for her feet,
And flickering hands to bruise the blossomy spray,
Treasure of light and tears and silver bloom;
And when she passes, pain and pity meet
Where all the white flowers faded into gray,
And all the blue flowers melted into gloom.

R. C.

The Spectator, CV (16 July 1910), 97.

The Death of the King.

The king is dead
On his golden bed,
His prayer is said
And his lesson read.

From pining for heaven,
And fear of the grave,
From taint and leaven
And lusts that enslave,
Now guards him well
A magic spell,
Like the fabled Seven
In their cave.

The world was his realm,
The sky his helm,
The sea his drink,
And blood his ink
To write his name
For deathless fame.

What did he write,
A word of delight,
Or a blot and blight
To add to the night
Of human woes?
What did he dare,
And whither fare
With the chainèd pair,
Hope and Despair?
Nobody knows.

He did many things,
As is meet for kings.
So many they were,
And felt so far,
That none can tell
If he did well.

He lived not long,
Yet was so strong
That he did more
Than men of fourscore
Who are not kings.
And some were glad
When he did die,
And some were sad
And heaved a sigh
For many things.

Such is the way
With kings, they say.
His name, you pray?
'Twas Yesterday.

R. T. CHANDLER.

The Westminster Gazette, XXXVII (4 January 1911), 2.

The Clay God.

Clay god, what brood'st thou in the dust and mould
Of this dark temple and deserted fane?
What wither'd fantasies of power old?
What ancient tales of mystery and pain?
What secrets that shall nevermore be told?
What phantoms that shall never walk again?

What music of a ghostly dulcimer,
Or chanting of a cowled spectre-priest
Hear'st thou in this old shrine where many a tear
Fell to thee once, and left thee unappeas'd?
Thou art forsaken of all human fear,
And from thee yearning hath forever ceas'd.

Deep-sunken is thy once far-glaring eye,
Where the years a vengeance on thy cunning wreak.
Sad moonbeams banish'd from the living sky
Lie on the curve of thy once sacred cheek,
Like wraiths of beauty that, when love is by,
Fall in the dust no more to move or speak.

Old blacken'd lamp-chains hang about thy head
Stirr'd by the swaying of a mournful breeze
That gropeth in thy kingdom of the dead
Some memory of a fair, lost day to seize,
Until it too in ruin cold is laid
And roams no more at any storm's decrees.

Brood on, with silence for the pale reward
And pardon of thy misty centuries!
Brood on, no thundrous battle may retard
Thy dusty rule and thy uncourted ease!
Brood on, thou hast no comfort for the bard
As from the terror of the night he flees!

For thee all kings on golden thrones that sit
Are as wan vapours of the twilight lone.
For thee desire is a lamp unlit,
And ages like to distant waters run.
Silent thou read'st the page which thou hast writ
Needing no eyes and careless of the sun.

R. T. CHANDLER.

The Westminster Gazette, XXXVII (9 February 1911), 2.

A Lament for Youth.

> From the forests of the night,
> From the palace of the day,
> He hath winged a distant flight;
> No more looms he on our sight,
> No more bows he to our sway.
> He was cunning in the mart,
> He was mighty with the sword,
> He was skilled in every art.
> Like a king he dwelt apart,
> And we fathomed not his word.
> Weep for him, each denizen
> Of the valley and the hill,
> Of the forest and the fen!
> For he cometh not again
> To our glory or our ill.
> Wake the echo of the lyre
> And the melody of song
> With a full and tragic fire!
> For our yearning shall not tire
> Till it mourneth sweet and long,
> Till the weary desert's verge
> And the shaggy mountain's head
> And the quiet-crooning surge
> Hear, and answer to the dirge
> Of our Youth that now is dead.

R. T. CHANDLER.

The Westminster Gazette, XXXVII (21 April 1911), 2.

The Unseen Planets.

Beyond the kingdom of the winking stars,
Beyond the silence of the ether deep,
Where memory, forgetting all its wars,
Lies down with death and life in dreamless sleep,
They ride majestic with attendant moons,
They swing like ships upon a perfect sea;
Through the procession of their nights and noons
Rack'd by what pain, fill'd with what mystery?
They are not told of in our feeble rote,
Nor mirror'd in our poor desire's face.
Where is the bard of melody remote
To hymn the glories of their mighty race?
    Beyond the fears, the faggots, and the rods,
    They wait,—new heavens with sublimer gods.

R. T. CHANDLER.

The Westminster Gazette, XXXVII (1 May 1911), 2.

The Tears That Sweeten Woe.

There is no thing in love or song
To match the tears that sweeten woe.
Not gems that deck the ornate throng
May meetly unto them belong,
But what the sage knows not, they know.

Not charmèd vision of romance
That rises like a god afar,
Yea, like a god of fiery glance
Who comes with golden sword and lance
Returning from a Titan war.

Not a still nook in nature's breast
Wherein the dreamer fitly dreams,
And where the soft leaves droop in rest
At evening's delicate behest
Wrapp'd in a mantle of moonbeams.

And not the dark, wind-haunted sea,
And not the stern and rugged hills,
The mists that follow eerily,
The moonlit groves of witchery,
The babble of the forest rills.

Nay, poet, seek not in your heart,
Nor in the lov'd one's eyes: in vain
Are all the fantasies of art;
From them the mysteries depart
To wait upon the tears of pain.

Lone is the road they take and long,
Gently they come, and gently go,
Far from the mart, far from the throng,
Far from desire, far from song,
The perfect tears that sweeten woe.

R. T. CHANDLER.

The Westminster Gazette, XXXVII (3 May 1911), 2.

The Fairy King.

Where the white owl guards the fir,
Where the woody silence falls,
Where the branches as they stir
Seem to lisp low madrigals,
There the fairy king is seen
On his throne of evergreen.

Where the brooklets coursing far
Musics choirless proclaim,
Tidings of a sylvan war,
Messages of rustic fame,
There the fairy king's commands
Travel to his loyal bands.

Where the hill-top greets the wind,
Rising from the sleep of earth,
And the hoary rock reclined
Dreams of buried tears and mirth,
There the fairy king goes up
With the queenly moon to sup.

Where the mossy cavern lies
Hidden in a nook of green,
And the jack-o'-lantern flies
Through the thicket lightly seen,
There the fairy king is laid
Sleeping in a dewy shade.

Where the foamy chargers stride
Out upon the windy deep,
Where the tempests in their pride

Spoils of mortal terror reap,
There he sails uncounted miles
To the far, enchanted isles.

Where the pale laburnums block
Sight unlawful from his porch,
And upon the quivering stalk
Climbs the glow-worm with his torch,
There he comes at night to hold
Levées of his chieftains bold.

Where the spectre-lights are lit
In the solemn caves of death,
And the misty mourners flit
Bearing many a cypress wreath,
There he lies in magic vault,
Casketed in ocean salt.

    R. T. CHANDLER.

The Westminster Gazette, XXXVII (16 June 1911), 2.

Untitled: "Arise, ye phantoms of delight . . ."

Arise, ye phantoms of delight, what time
    The fire low burneth,
Ye freaks of melody and sorry rhyme
    That memory spurneth,
Ye echoes of old songsters dim, forlorn,
    And plaintive magic,
Fast-sepulchred between the night and morn,
    Yet little tragic!

Ye shall not move unto the sound of dirge
    Or muffled bell,
Nor be confounded with despair's dark surge
    And wild sea-knell.
Pale-eyed and mantled with the dust of years,
    Awake to pleasure,
And, drying up those dim, unheeded tears,
    Come, trip a measure!

Now when small grasses whisper and are bold,
    And winds are straying
Down in the beech-grove where the fairies hold
    Their midnight maying,
Now when the wizard opes his evil books
    And goblin screed,
Come forth, O sprites, from you forgotten nooks
    And take your meed!

Ye shall not have the tinkle of the stars
    Unto your dancing,
Ye shall not come as from immortal wars,
    With armour glancing,

But if the gods have touched my heart with song
  Or any fire,
Ye shall not lack a tune to linger long
  Upon the lyre.

And through the patches of entrancing light
  The late flame throweth,
Wreathed like pale forget-me-nots of night,
  The day not knoweth,
Ye shall dance on until the dawning red
  Gilds the high towers,
And every fairy hastens to his bed
  Of wild wood flowers.

R. T. CHANDLER.

The Westminster Gazette, XXXVIII (15 November 1911), 2.

An Old House.

Sing, whoso will, of smoothest lawn,
Trim hedges, and of posies neat,
But I will wake the ashy dawn
In some old garden by the street,
Behind some ancient rusty wall,
Where far-flung creepers catch the rain,
And where the slateless eaves are tall
Above the dusty window-pane.

And I will hear an old gate swing
To autumn winds that sob and moan,
And I will hear the thrushes sing
Upon a cracking seat of stone.
Let spiders' webs hang in the trees,
Whose stretching fingers mock the sky,
And I will chant old mysteries
As in an arbour dark I lie.

The raindrop symphony shall sound
Along the barely boarded rooms,
And in damp cellars shall be found
A treasure-house of goblin glooms.
Behind a black and rusty door
Fantastic shades shall hold me still,
And, playing to a silent score,
My heart with wizard airs shall fill.

And I shall hear the city die
Far off, as over pathless seas,
And see the ghosts of memory
Play over their pale obsequies,
As through the twilit rooms I go,
Or watch the dusty sunbeams dance,
While Melancholia guides me slow
The willing captive of Romance.

R. T. CHANDLER.

The Westminster Gazette, XXXIX (1 March 1912), 2.

The King.

The night doth cut with shadowy knife
In half the kingdom of the sun;
The red dawn meets with her in strife;—
Vassal of mine I hold each one.

The sailors chant beside the mast,
The tempests lash the riven foam,
But I, the King, am striding fast
Before the prow, to guide it home.

I am the lover wed to tears,
I am the cynic cold and sage,
I am the ghost of noble years,
I am the prophet lapp'd in rage.

I am the fane no longer trod
That moulders on the wild hill-brow;
I am the fresh and radiant god
To whom the young religions bow.

Perfection woo'd in many a guise
Is in my charge, a stabled beast;
The myriad moons look from my eyes;
The worlds unnam'd sit at my feast.

My glance is in the splendid noon,
The golden orchid blown of heat;
My brow is as the South lagoon,
And all the stars are at my feet.

The lost waves moan: I made their song.
The lost lands dream: I wove their trance.
The earth is old, and death is strong;
Stronger am I, the true Romance.

R. T. CHANDLER.

The Westminster Gazette, XXXIX (25 April 1912), 2.

Time Shall Not Die.

How shall he die who walked the sky
    Ere the first wild sun uprose?
How shall he pass who trod the grass
    When the first bud did unclose?
Who was long ere the moon grew fair
    A lord of many lands,
Shall he not reign o'er hill and plain
    When Earth hath folded her hands?

How shall he be a memory
    In the wine of a later feast,
Or a grief outgrown that stirs at dawn
    From the gate of a wider East?
How shall he rest a shrine unblest,
    A changeful heart's decoy,
When the laughing page of a far-off age
    Shall cast a moment's joy?

Likelier when all the clarions call
    Adown the lists of death,
And every knight comes riding light
    Helm'd in a cypress wreath,
When all the hosts are mantled ghosts
    And all the kings are gone,
Still shall there one outlive the sun,
    And watch the pageant on.

No phantom he of ecstasy,
    Perfume on some old glove,
No whisper'd song that once rang strong

From the lips of Minstrel Love;
No scratching mouse in a ruin'd house,
  No raindrip down the wall,
But a king of fear with a sable spear,
  A monarch wise and tall.

And when the old pale creeds are cold,
  And all their gods are dust,
And life far on chanting is gone
  To seek another lust,
Time shall be left, a lord bereft
  Of lands but not of life,
To tell his wars to silent stars
  That are full tir'd of strife.

Wraith-roses white shall bloom by night
  In avenues of gloom,
And small fire-flies with spectral eyes
  Shall light the dead earth's tomb,
When the book is read and the lesson said,
  And the song is sungen out;
And Time alone shall guard his throne,
  Lord of the silent rout.

R. T. CHANDLER.

Unlocated.

Organic Music.[2]

Starlight adrift on the Ionian sea,
Slow, heavy mutter of the antique mass,
Or rustle of the boughs in Arcady,
Or furlèd lilies nodding in a pass;
Rains of the black night where the lost souls plead,
Pure fugues from the long litany of love,
Or swoop of plovers to the swaying reed,
Or perfum'd lyrics from an Eastern grove,—
   These are but visions, sounds and single notes
   That tremble from the organ's hundred throats.

Yea, I have heard the moaning violin,
Long-drawn emotion too intense for thought,
Heard, too, the clumsy trombone blundering in,
A gaping rustic in a holy spot,
Heard, too, the frail celeste whose bells are caught
Like tinkling ice-drops in a net of mist,
Heard, too, the melancholy 'cello, fraught
With all vain griefs that elegy hath kiss'd.
   Time was I loved them well: now let them rest,
   For second loves like second thoughts are best.

Yea, I have heard the scratch of poets' pens,
And seen the Buddha's calm, eternal smile,
And watch'd the arrows in the green Ardennes,
And mark'd the shadows down the peristyle,
And these were well. But richer dreams are press'd

Out of thy heart, god of the hollow pipe,
God of the golden vineyard on whose breast
The dark wine of elysium groweth ripe,
    Lull'd by the thunder of the swinging tides
    On that far isle where ecstasy abides.

                    R. T. CHANDLER.

CHANDLER BEFORE

ESSAYS AND
SKETCHES:
1911-1912

MARLOWE

The Academy, 19 August 1911, p. 250.

The Genteel Artist

Perhaps there was once a day when the artist was a man of toil, capable of vying in industry with the farm labourer and of excelling him in most things else. One likes, for example, to think of those mediæval gilders and carvers and stainers as sitting all day from dawn till dusk by leaded panes in queer old silent houses, plying their tasks with relentless perseverance, careless of the weather and the antics of history. One likes to think of them taking frugal meals beside their work, munching an apple while putting the finishing touches to a gilded devil, holding the tankard with one hand and the brush with the other. One feels sure that when the night came they went to bed with a very pleasant weariness, slept soundly, and did not lie awake wondering how they had managed to foozle at the eighth green. No doubt their pleasures were simple; and the invention of some slight artistic device was the joy of many weeks. They lived quiet lives and died quiet deaths, leaving behind them arts which we mimic with a vain superficiality. No doubt, like all enthusiasts, they were capable of quarrelling violently over very small details. No doubt they were on occasion careless of their morals, and rather neglected to arrange the universe and to populate Valhalla according to their private moods. They had their faults, being human; but when we turn from them to their successors of these days, how very favourable to them is the comparison! How very garish seem the surroundings of the prosperous ladies and gentlemen who paint our successful pictures and write our successful books; the pleasant people who sit in padded chairs before mahogany writing-tables, wielding gold-banded fountain pens or dictating in a leisurely manner over a choice cigar or cigarette!

There appeared once, in one of those popular articles on contemporary painters which have long been a feature of a certain magazine, the portrait of a gentleman standing elegantly before the easel upon which one of his own creations reposed. A spotless silk handkerchief peeped from his pocket, his cuffs were stiff and white as if they had only just left the haberdasher's, his beard was as trim as an aristocratic shrubbery, the crease in his trousers was perfect, the cut of his coat ideal, the radiance of his shoes all that dreams could desire. He had a negligent air, as of being about to do something interesting with a perfect ease and politeness. A cigarette drooped from the corner of his mouth, and his half-closed eyes seemed more intent upon the floating smoke than on anything else in this transient world. In the background were rich curtains and expensive furniture. Beneath his feet was a thick carpet upon which presumably no spot of paint had ever fallen. And the sum total of one's idea of this gentleman was that he was in no danger of producing a great painting. He might be a charming companion, he was more than well-groomed, and he was very possibly more than usually clever. But the beholder felt quite sure that he was not a great artist. He had never felt the sweet bitterness of the garret, he had never dreamed a day away on a hillside, he had never shuddered at a vision or wept over a fantastic sorrow. Or, if he had, at a simpler age, done any of these things, the experience had left no mark, and had not made him any more cunning in his work.

The story goes, it is true, of one great painter of a past century who always attired himself for his easel as if for a fashionable gathering, in the stiffest of ruffs, the richest of velvet, and the most costly lace. And it is easy to sympathise with his attitude. He looked upon his art as something to be attempted only in a perfect purity of mind and body; he clad himself for his work as the bride for her wedding or the young girl for her first Communion. And if any such sentiment was present in the breasts of our modern genteel artists and writers, one could welcome it and approve. But to them their art is a business or a whim or a side issue of some sort, a thing to do for a couple of hours in the evening before dinner. It would never be permitted to interfere with a social function or a motor-excursion. It would never cause its devotees to miss a meal or to bundle a friend out of the room with a vigorous rudeness. It would never produce exhaustion or the sweat of a terrible toil. Its creators do not weep like Dickens over their imaginary deathbeds nor tremble like Poe at the horror of their own visions. They do not sit for impotent hours over a blank sheet, nor revile all created things because they cannot attain the impossible. So far from being a religion their art is scarce even a profession; it is merely an exercise. They may gather fortunes, but they are never more than dilettanti, and the poorest hack of Grub-street or the most utterly forgotten carver of Ghent is their better.

Art is not the be-all and end-all even of this present life, and it is possible for the artist to take himself and his work far too seriously. One would not have every poet and painter possessed of devils; but surely a touch of fanaticism makes for great achievement. Art has, in these days, real and apparent enemies which it never had in ages of infinitely less widespread culture, and the artist who aspires to the meagrely-rewarded success of true distinction will get through the easier if he be lightly touched with fanaticism. Nothing in a man of character breeds this healthy fanaticism more certainly than a little hardship and want of luxury. Other things being equal, one feels that a great poem is more likely to be written on a deal table than on an article of inlaid rosewood. The genius in the garret may have an uncomfortable time in many ways, but he has one great advantage over his more luxurious rivals—he is compelled to throw himself body and soul into his work. He must live with it entirely. All moods and all hours must contribute their inspiration to it, all sensations of the mind and body must wait upon it, every thought and impression must carve some line, however faint, in its ideal structure. The night spreads her wings about it, all the colours of the sun light it up, all the noises of the city, all the voices of Nature are somehow echoed in it. It lies as close to life as any work of man may lie, and in the result, be it failure or success, it has not lacked attention. The garreteer, whether he eventually dies famous or completely un-known, has been worthy of his craft. But the genteel artist, in his expensive study or studio, smiled upon by electric lights, flattered by costly mirrors, embraced by Russia-leather chairs, can seldom make any such claim. His successes are usually mere *tours de force*, like juggling with billiard balls, noteworthy only because they amuse and because not everyone can imitate them. He turns out a novel or a painting as neatly and as coldly as the machine turns out the packed ounce of tobacco, and probably in the general scheme of things the three products are of similar value.

R. T. CHANDLER.

The Academy, 9 September 1911, p. 322.

The Remarkable Hero

The time is not distant beyond the memory of living men when the hero of a typical novel had to be, if not a person of title, at any rate a man of tolerable family. If, in the days of his affluence, he did not possess a valet, or if when leaving home under a cloud he could not bestow his last sovereign on a head gardener, he was not likely to have many admirers. The snobbishness of those days was not greater than the snobbishness of these, but it was far simpler and more straightforward. It demanded quite honestly, on behalf of the middle-class reader, to mix with its social betters. No doubt it was perfectly right; if a man cannot choose his company even in novels things are in a bad way. But, however that may be, the distinction of the hero of that time was on the side of birth and breeding. He might be compelled by circumstances to associate with coalheavers, but even when his coat was shiny at the elbows the cabmen called him "My lord." When he told the landlady of his humble lodging that he had come into a marquisate and forty thousand a year, she always reminded him that she had known him at the first for a "real gent." His brains might be of feeble quality—indeed they usually were—but his manners were of the best. He might not know how to counter the most childish plot, but he invariably knew what to do with his hands in a drawing-room, a problem which has puzzled more people than ever troubled about the riddles of life and death.

In these days, however, good breeding is usually left as a minor perquisite to the villain. The hero may, as far as his social position is concerned, be anybody. He may drop his aspirates, he may be a boor, he may be ignorant of the most elementary rules of polite behaviour. Common honesty is not in the least a necessity to him. If he is fiendishly ugly, his adventures are all the more piquant. He may even be deformed, and his Life will sell in tens of thousands. He may squint, he may be club-footed, he may wear ready-made clothes, he may smoke in church, he may shoot foxes, he may browbeat women and patronise old men, he may do any of those forbidden things, for doing the least of which we would cut our dearest friends, and yet he may charm voracious multitudes. We care nothing for his clothes, nor his manners nor his antecedents nor his actions; in these respects we are all-tolerant. But there is one quality which we demand in him: he must be a remarkable person. It matters very little in what his fate lies, whether in art, finance, sport, politics, exploration, swindling, or throat-cutting, but his intellect must be of the cast of great men.

The superficial reason is not very far to seek. Satirised out of his old, honest, matter-of-fact reverence for rank and wealth, the commonplace reader has to satisfy his inborn humility by looking up to an intellectual superior. Forbidden to act the flunkey to the aristocrat, he allows himself to adore the prima donna, the brilliant statesman, the swaggering freebooter, or the subtle master of intrigue. As he can no longer delight in the conversation of a duke, he accepts instead the conversation of an eminent house-breaker. And seeing that, however slight his knowledge of aristocratic circles might have been, his acquaintance with men of genius is even slighter—he is seldom able to detect the fraud which is so often played upon him. He may have a shrewd conception of how a duke would behave in a given situation, but a man of genius is above laws, and his actions are therefore incalculable. So the reader takes, with shut eyes and open mouth, whatever the journeyman novelist cares to offer him in the way of inspired heroes. He is unaware that the great detective whom he so much admires is as unlike any possible great detective as he is unlike a Patagonian anteater; these mysterious and incomprehensible actions pass not, as they should, for the well-meaning, but rather futile, efforts of an uninspired writer to simulate inspiration, but for the unfathomable deeds of a demigod. The more extraordinary they are, the more convinced is the reader of his hero's genuineness. In the result, one reads of a great realistic author who studies his situations by kidnapping people, and forcing them to act for him; one finds a great thief who lives, surrounded by *objets d'art*, in a castle in the middle of a sea-girt rock; one finds a great poet who, by way of seeking inspiration, wanders like a madman over the face of the earth for several months, then, returning home, scribbles for four days without stopping, and finally falls dead over his completed masterpiece. The convenience for a second-rate author of a public which accepts such creations may easily be estimated. If extravagance be a sign of genius, then it is infinitely easier to portray genius than mediocrity. The man in the street is quite capable of judging his kind, but to judge the weird antics of an inspired soul he has only the unreliable experience of nightmares. He can but devour and hold out his innocent hands for more. So the curious fashion grows, until the remarkable becomes more common than the commonplace; an amusing development enough, if one does not pause to reflect how swiftly this highly-seasoned fare can destroy any lingering taste for the products of a restrained and disciplined art.

[Unsigned]

The Academy, 4 November 1911, p. 560.

The Literary Fop

There is a type of literary person, known to all periods, who bears something of the same relation to literature as the fop bears to manners. As the fop lives only to indicate certain poses and gesturings of life, so the exquisite of literature writes only to extract quaint flavours and essences which are accidental to Art, and not of its true spirit. Like the beau, he is apt to be a leader of fashion; like the beau, he is a stranger to the multitude, and a bugbear to simple, intelligent folk, and possesses an exquisite sensibility in matters which are unimportant. So great is this sensibility that he resents the carelessness of those whom he vaguely knows to be his betters; so regardless is he of the deep questions that lie behind all Art that he cannot understand any preoccupation save that with the superficial. A writer lax in his periods, though of sublime imagination, is to the literary fop like a person in a shabby coat. He may be a good fellow at heart, but it behoves him to change his tailor before seeking the society of gentlemen.

The literary fop is perhaps most common in times of mild and not unpleasant reaction—the less vital a literature the greater its refinement. When not under the necessity of fighting at the barricades, it can afford to loll in rose-gardens and toy with Watteau fans. Then is the hour of the fop. He mimics the battles of heroes with a toy sword; he repeats the declamations of fierce orators in silky tones and sentences of luxurious elaboration. He refines over and over upon the technique of the masters, because technique is his entire preoccupation; he overcomes the gods at decorative games because they play them with careless eyes and minds pondering on other things, while to him they are the sum of existence. He lays down the canons of a minute art which might possibly amuse the Olympians on an idle afternoon, but can have no real connection with the business of a laborious world. In the end, as often as not, he dies lamenting the coarseness of the world's most cunning craftsmen. Thus he is apt to be a pessimist—self-taught, condemned to seek in vain, as the one light of life, what the wise discard as will-o'-the-wisps of intellectual debauchery.

Like all pleasant and unimportant things, the creed of the literary fop moves much in fashions, from courtly love-song to chivalric romance, from pastoral heroics to symbolism, from the recondite conceits of sonneteers to high-flown analysis of exotic religions. No doubt these fashions have been largely the backwash of true schools of art; at any rate, we hear little of them in the most detailed histories of literature. Since they are not so easily and emphatically distinguished from vital movements as, for instance, extravagant fashions are from the natural evolution of clothes, and are not, on the other hand, accepted, like the costume of past ages, as matters of antiquarian interest, they have lacked their special historian. We know little of them beyond our own memories, though we seem to detect them broadcast in our reading, and may argue for ever as to where they begin and end. We hear their echoes and feel their dim and not always unwholesome presence throughout all literature, but they are seldom more than ghosts, far too vague for classification. They have cast many a false glamour over learning, and made the reputation of many a superfluous poet or critic.

But if we distinguish the literary fop with difficulty in the past, we can observe him at our leisure in the present. His work is all about us. In fiction he is powerful, in *belles lettres* he is all but supreme. We can see the touch of his hand in half of the output of eclectic journalism; he is responsible for many tones in latter-day criticism; poetry is all but entirely beneath his sway; he holds in his hands most of the canons of the complete essayist. Even in humour, which was not always his strong point, he has obtained firm footing. But this spreading of his reign in an age which, in spite of its faults, is not so much decadent as reactionary, is due to another cause. As he was once the product of refined idleness, he is now, paradoxically enough, a phenomenon of the sheer hard struggle for life among the appallingly numerous people who are authors without any particular justification. When men have no message which they burn to utter, and yet find themselves compelled to write day by day, they speedily develop those idiosyncrasies of outlook and manner which are the hall-mark of the literary fop. Being without any true originality, they make some unneeded refinement their substitute, offering half-tones instead of colours, forms instead of ideas, verbiage instead of words, and moods instead of theories. They sweep up the dust of big movements and display it as stuff of their own minds. They catch the unconsidered trifles of current philosophy and twist them into tremendous mysteries. They are often plagiarists, and not seldom thieves, but they work as hard for their meagre output as the most laborious of true artists for their masterpieces. The harm they do is in the futile complication of literary craftmanship, and in the bewilderment of simple folk in search of truth. It might be added that they bar the way of better writers than themselves, but that is true of the second-rate in all departments of life.

What will be the end of them it is impossible to say. They have seen the fall of more than one Empire, but it does not follow that they will see the fall of yet another; the modern world has a miraculous power of absorbing cranks. In the meantime they help to make the consideration of contemporary literature an impossibility to busy folk; they employ the publishers and they madden the casual, sensible reader. They have done their best to make authorship commonplace and art a matter of formulas. Their declamations fill the market place, and turn Grub Street into a Tower of Babel. It is curious to reflect that their predecessors were once indolent triflers in drawing-rooms.

R. T. C.

The Academy, 6 January 1912, p. 5.

Realism and Fairyland

Fairyland is Everyman's dream of perfection, and changes, dreamlike, with the mood of the dreamer. For one it is a scene of virgin, summery Nature undefiled by even the necessary works of man. For another it is a place where there exist no codes, conventions, or moral laws, and where people love or hate at sight, having their virtues and vices writ large upon them. For another it is a champaign dotted with fine castles, in which live sweet ladies clad in silk, spinning, and singing as they spin, and noble knights who do courteous battle with each other in forest glades; or a region of uncanny magic, haunting music, elves and charmed airs and waters. For still another it may be an anarchy of the beautiful touched with terror, tenanted by spirits who must be propitiated with cakes left on the window-sill and soft words spoken up the chimney at night. No two minds see fairyland alike or demand like gifts from it, and to the same fancy it alters from day to day, as the winds change which blow about a house, and with as little apparent reason. Nevertheless it gives by contraries so accurate a reflection of life that the spirit of an age is more essentially mirrored in its fairy-tales than in the most painstaking chronicle of a contemporary diarist.

The visions of what is called idealism are only reflections of fairyland and its experiences; they share with the scenes of that wonderful domain the merit of telling the truth about those who see them, and of telling it the more clearly because unconsciously. Yet there have arisen in the last half-century, more or less, certain long-faced, earnest, intent, and seemingly very daring people, who inform us sadly that we must look dull facts in the face if we would see truth, that we must not delude ourselves with rosy dreams or golden castles in Spain. By way of showing us how to proceed they rake over the rubbish-heaps of humanity in its close alleys and noisome slums to find fragments of broken moral crockery, to nose out the vices of unfortunate people, to set upon them the worst possible interpretation for the social system, and, by the simple process of multiplication, to construct from them what they consider typical human beings. Determining to hide nothing, and to show every side of life impartially, they forget that the things which necessarily strike them most in their impartial survey and appear most emphatic in their work are mere offal of the senses; as a man with a delicate sense of smell would find unpleasant odours the chief feature of life in a hovel of disease. Boldly declaring that they will cast aside all factitious optimism, they automatically choose the dark aspect of all things in order to be on the safe side; as a result unpleasantness becomes associated in their minds with truth, and if they wish to produce a faultlessly exact portrait of a man, all they need do is to paint his weaknesses and then, for the sake of propitiating the instinct of kindness left by some oversight in their hearts, to explain that his shortcomings are the inevitable consequences of a mistaken scheme of life. There remains only to set down the man thus portrayed in a *milieu*, the dulness, sordidness, and stuffiness of which is "reproduced" with a monotonous and facile elaboration hitherto unknown in art, and a masterpiece of realism is obtained. It is hardly surprising that when such stuff is given to tired and overworked men and women with unsteady nerves as a study for their leisure hours, it is apt to cause a certain flavour of despondency and pessimism to become characteristic of the time, with the social result that if any difficult problem of life clamours to be solved those best equipped for solving it have utterly lost all youthful hope and cheer and have no energy for the labour. They pass on with sighs, leaving the task to bureaucrats and party politicians.

It is an old sneer, no doubt, that realism is a picker-up of life's refuse, and it may be just that any point of view which belongs to a large class of people should find representation in art. But it has never been proved to the satisfaction of the most reasonable and easily convinced visionary that the realistic is a definite point of view. For in truth it is only the mood of every man's dull and depressed hours. We are all realists at times, just as we are all sensualists at times, all liars at times, and all cowards at times. And if it be urged that for this very reason, because it is human, realism is essential to art, the obvious answer comes, that this claim entitles it at most to a niche in the temple, not as at present to a domination of the whole ritual, and that truth in art, as in other things, should not be sought by that process of exhaustion encouraged so fatally in our age by the pedants of science, and by their fallacy that it may be discovered by considering all the possibilities: a method which surrenders intuition and all the soul's fine instincts to receive in exchange a handful of theories, which, compared with the infinite forms of immortal truth known to the gods, are as a handful of pebbles to a thousand miles of shingly beach.

Faulty as its philosophy is, however, the realistic creed which dominates our literature is not due so much to bad theories as to bad art. To be an idealist one must have a vision and an ideal; to be a realist, only a plodding, mechanical eye. Of all forms of art realism is the easiest to practise, because of all forms of mind the dull mind is commonest. The most unimaginative or uneducated person in the world can describe a dull scene dully, as the worst builder can produce an ugly house. To those who say that there are artists, called realists, who produce work which is neither ugly nor dull nor painful, any man who has walked down a commonplace city street at twilight, just as the lamps are lit, can reply that such artists are not realists, but the most courageous of idealists, for they exalt the sordid to a vision of magic, and create pure beauty out of plaster and vile dust.

R. T. C.

The Academy, 20 January 1912, p. 84.

The Tropical Romance

The tropical romance appears to be doomed; its sacred domain has been invaded, and its fiery hearth desecrated, by cold bands of Northern realists. No longer are the vivid colours, hot lights, and dancing blue seas its inalienable property, nor the dreamy Southern stars and phosphorescent wakes of South-bound whalers. No longer does it glide majestically by glorious palm-fringed islands bathed in opalescent light, pant over burning ageless deserts, insinuate itself through the tangled mysterious bazaars of the Orient, or have strange dealings with grave Arabs, smiling Kanakas, inscrutable Chinamen, wily Japanese.

Gone, too, are its heroes, the strong men who look unmoved on death and horror, picturesque, hard-living cynics of the high seas and barbaric lands, lean as tigers, weather-beaten as figure-heads, clad in weird garments, and smoking eternal cheroots. Life amid these entrancing scenes and people has grown less simple. Its plain-spoken monarchs have given way to smug heroes who are neat storehouses of psychological lore, displayed at leisure by patient analysts, in whose hands the pirate appears cockney and the primal typhoon explains itself like the long-winded introducer of a private bill. The very savage is grown a person of more mental complication than the enlightened European of a century back, and his careless hut is one of the stages whereon athletic realists exercise their dreary gifts. Under this reign there is no room for the adventurer, artless and incorrigible. He is driven from his kingdom, and has no land to call his own. He lurks no man knows where, lamenting the golden past. A few of his kind only, and those the degenerate ones, have not scorned to set foot in cities, where they bow and strut in Brummagem-made clockwork detective stories, and may possibly appear heroic to errand-boys.

No doubt the development is largely a matter of geography. The touch of strangeness, the sense of exploration has vanished from those far-off, dangerous, inaccessible regions once loved by violent adventure. The remote corners of the earth draw nearer and nearer, until they are almost at our doorsteps, and we look out of our front windows on all the races of mankind. Local colour, however burning, is to be bought at a few shillings the page from any literary hack. The vivid romantic settings have been tabulated and indexed, and there is no more exhilaration in coming upon one of them than in choosing an apple from a fruit-dish. As far as fiction is concerned, they are but as Brixton villas and Mayfair drawing-rooms, commonplaces of which every one knows all that he wishes to know.

Certainly the violent romance of the tropics had its faults. It did not paint life as season-ticket-holders see it. It was apt to display the raw red edge of things, and to provide murderous-minded authors with a great many opportunities to enlarge on the surgical aspect of sudden death. It did not increase one's love for the suburban back garden, the measured plot in which the City clerk may pace on Sundays and holidays, and tell himself that his house is his castle. Its alarmingly swift justice did not cause one to admire the vacillating movements of political reform, nor did its somewhat vulgar insistence on the maxim that the heroic attitude of life covers a multitude of sins appeal to æsthetic young people who had just discovered themselves to be in the intellectual vanguard of the times. The tropical romance was inclined, in short, to lay too much emphasis on the gladiatorial virtues, and to hint too much contempt for those polite shrinkings which, when accompanied by a knowledge of ancient literature and a knack for artistic rhapsody, often pass as the most subtle philosophy. Nevertheless, to it belonged, in its day, the magic of the places where life is a mighty colourist, and it made that magic live as no other literature has ever done. And they were men, those somewhat shop-soiled heroes with tarnished morals and unflinching courage. One is forced to lament their passing, even if one could improve upon their ethics, and the lament is not so much because there is fear of a lack of brave men to succeed them as because there may at least be honest doubt whether the morbid, introspective heroes of the analytical school, or the passion-fettered pawns of the sexual realists, are as wise ideals for the novel-reading public. Perhaps the new heroes have the advantage of being easier to get rid of, if they are acknowledged to be obnoxious; for the heroes of the tropical romance were not killed without a struggle. And it might possibly be urged that their savagery and imperviousness to ideas were as firm barriers to progress as the worst decadence and the most vicious misuse of passion.

Our acceptance or denial of that view depends on the value which we attach to romance. It depends on whether we believe that heaven were better won in fighting inch by inch up the slopes of Olympus, or by the noiseless, strifeless working of a machine. It depends on whether one is a philanthropist in the sense of desiring to spare men pain and discomfort, or in the sense of longing to create for them such enthusiasm as will overcome all pain and all discomfort. It depends, in fine, on whether the best way is the line of least resistance or the rocky path of great endeavour, whether we are to be saved by the science or by the poetry of life. And that, after all, is the typical question of the age.

R. T. C.

The Academy, 24 February 1912, pp. 248–49.

Houses To Let

There are some old houses, never too charming in the days of
their prosperity, when their windows were full of light, when
their passages resounded with the footsteps of commonplace
people, and their walls gave back the echoes of dull conversation, that in age and neglect seem to be halfway houses of pure
romance. They are to be found in most suburbs, in back streets
where, for one of a dozen reasons, house property is at a low
ebb, nooks and corners of villadom situated at an unbusiness-
like distance from railway-stations, places of badly-lighted
streets and unmended roads. One may perambulate more popular quarters for hours with a feeling of depression at the evidence everywhere of the paramount *bourgeois* spirit, seeing
through front windows the inevitable delf bowl on a *table
d'occasion*, the outlines of laboured family portraits, the most
recent improvements in gas-fittings or electric light shining
hardly on those clean, smug bookcases, which seem to cry aloud
that they have as little as possible to do with literature or learning. In the gardens one sees the usual round bed with the
carefully-reared geraniums in the middle, the trim hedge cut
weekly, the gravel path with an edge as straight as that of a
piece of notepaper, the whitened steps, and the resplendent
door-knocker. Passing by these shows comes some grass-grown
roadway, haunted by a dilapidated mansion, once, no doubt, a
desirable residence, but now roughened by neglect into some
deeper thing. There will be a crazy iron gateway, perhaps, lean-
ing away from its posts, its two parts held in precarious communion by a rusty chain. There will be a mossy path, a flight of
dirty steps, leading to a blackened door, a few frowning, cob-
webbed windows, a lofty, unkempt hedge, and perhaps two or

three rose-bushes which still, if it is summer, put forth stunted blooms through the coils of serpent-like creepers. That and no more; yet what a door this poor *ensemble* opens to the imagination! The effect is like that of a fine etching, colourless but full of suggestion, with a faint flavour of the sordid—but it is the romance of sordidness.

One never thinks of such a house as quite human in the comfortable bread-and-butter sense. It is rather like an untidy outpost of fairyland; every loss from the domestic neatness is a gain, every touch of dilapidation a new evidence of enchantment. If the windows are dusty, the more fit are they to frame goblin faces peering forth at midnight. If the door is cracked and its knocker corroded, the more naturally might it resound to the ghostly rat-tat of a magician. If the roof has lost many slates, so that one can hear the raindrops echoing from room to room on wet days, the more such an accompaniment fits that higher melancholy which is the half of beauty.

It is likely enough that the house will front a rectangular garden, sodden grass plots and lost-looking trees. But looking from the front one can never quite rid oneself of the idea that it conceals a lovingly arranged pleasure-ground, which has somehow escaped the eye of the jerry-builder, a kingdom of ruin whose dimensions have somehow evaded the mathematics of ground space; an unknown region where the grass climbs waist-high and leans over the paths to form a tunnel, through which an adventurous child might creep for an hour and never see the sun; where there lingers a grey sundial half overwhelmed by encroaching jungle, a mimic Greek altar before which he might burn matches as incense to the outlandish gods of childhood; where there is entered by stooping beneath a pall of ivy a decrepit summer-house, whose interior is hot and dark at noon, and its one window a blind eye veiled by a closely-woven tapestry of creeper-stems. There may be, too, a quiet orchard where all through the months of fruit the leaves rustle dryly as the birds swing on the hanging pears and apples. There may be invisible rockeries lying in wait to tumble the invader into a warm bed of couch-grass, and high walls with stone copings, work of the days when private property was still an unshaken idol. So much is not a great deal to ask, but the finding is doubtful, and it is wiser to stay in the road and peer through the rusty gates.

Who has not, when looking at those landscapes and interiors of the Dutch School, been haunted by a longing to adventure ever so little beyond where the picture ends, to glance through some half-opened door or to round the turn of some charming path? It is much the same with our empty house. It is not only because what one sees is magical, but also because it is so little, that one is filled with a desire of what lies beyond. But the wise man goes away with the desire in his heart, content with that cameo which Nature, battling, like the idealist, with an ugly civilisation, has achieved for him. He knows, too, that even could he find such a garden as he imagines, and penetrate to its end, he would still ache to climb the wall and discover new realms of lonely enchantment. And perhaps he would burst through some protesting door to behold a railway-cutting or the vista, not poetically distant, of a line of workmen's cottages. Then the domain would shrink, the ugliness of suburban life would batter upon its frontiers, and he would turn sadly away, like that man who thought he held a priceless jewel in his hand, and, opening his fingers to examine it, found a morsel of dry bread.

R. T. CHANDLER.

The Academy, 29 June 1912, pp. 817–18.

The Phrasemaker

He whom we may without impertinence call the Phrasemaker is not one of the violent protagonists of literature. He has not shouted in triumph upon the mountain-top nor fled shrieking through the haunted wood. He has but little idea of the depth and vividness of life, concerns himself a great deal with trifles, and hardly has it in him to do justice to a memorable catastrophe. We cannot imagine him at war with the gods of civilisation, perched in a sixth-floor garret, cramped over a bare wooden table, tousled and feverish, spattering his fingers with ink and his soul with dæmonic dreams. We cannot see him roaming the city, black-browed and anarchistic, growling behind an enormous pipe, and sneering beneath the lamp-post at the passing personified follies of life. He does not sit up until strange hours of the midnight nor arrange his meals in a fantastic schedule. He is as regular in his habits as an archdeacon; he shaves and has his boots blacked. One might set a clock by him without risk of serious error; seldom does he allow his breakfast to grow cold in waiting. He is a commonplace person, a product of ease and study, of quiet desires and facile happiness.

He sits by the fire with a pad of paper upon his knee and reviews the pageant of the coals, or by an open window in summer he draws sentiment from the evening and sets it upon paper in a perfume of fine language. He proceeds with deliberation in his work, has a neat handwriting, holds pen or pencil just so and seldom makes a false start, since, before putting a stroke on the paper, he has gone through a whole elaborate ritual of choice and arrangement. His greatest doubt is to be torn between two phrases seemingly equal in point of beauty; then will he wander from one to the other like a devoted gardener among his roses, touching a flower of language here and there, smiling and putting his head on one side in a critical attitude. In his greatest triumph he is restrained; his pen moves no faster over his darling sentence than that of an engrosser over the title of a deed. He seems rather to emblazon than to write his words, forming his letters as if they themselves were to appear for the world to read and were not destined to be thrust aside by a torrent of vulgar leaden type.

In thought the Phrasemaker is apt to be superficial, for he finds the exact arrangement of small things so fascinating that he can take little interest in the rough-hewing of large questions. And this superficiality is as much an intention as an effect; in his creed the word is as mighty as the thought, humanly speaking, and he who can form a perfect sentence has in him the power to produce a perfect book. The many examples to the contrary the Phrasemaker lays at the door of carelessness, to remove which from literary language is his aim and ambition. Towards that goal he marches with steady gaze and even tread; nothing can turn him aside from his path. Even ridicule, being a thing less exquisite than that which on his part calls it forth, is negligible to him. If he is not a fanatic, it is because his method forbids any extreme save that of beauty, which after all is not an extreme but a golden mean. He is the perfect man of letters; compared with him all others are but amateur or professional authors. He alone has no thought unconnected with literature.

To this man comes bitter as death the assertion that art is merely an adjunct of sociology. For him words and phrases live a perfect life of their own, and should not be plagued by outside interference. They dwell in a land of visions into which Poor Law Reports, Statistics of Birth and Marriage and other official documents enter only to scatter ruin. The brutal, mercenary and vulgar sides of life the Phrasemaker shrinks from by instinct, and it is probable that he sees a certain coarseness in the God who permits them. He is not intimate with either heaven or earth as they are seen by the mass of men; he has fashioned his own battle-ground and his own chosen Nirvana from one single ideal and activity.

In the end he comes to see most things through a veil of fine language. Nature becomes for him a box of many small compartments containing colours and tints and tones, from among which he selects the most beautiful and weaves them into a pattern of his own design. Whether that design has any ultimate meaning or no does not concern the Phrasemaker; he judges it by its appeal to his own conception of beauty. There is thus a touch of ineffectuality about him, for he will not take his subject-matter as it comes, and embroider both the mud-puddles and the rose-gardens of life into his art. He insists upon selecting and refining; he has a horror of decadence, which robuster minds rather incline to view as a tasty morsel in the varied feast of art. He shuts his eyes to everything but perfection; he handles language like a diamond-cutter's tool, and will not employ it to slice Dutch cheese or black bread. He is blameless in his intentions, but often absurd in his scruples. He is behind the times, a phantom of another age who still wanders pensively in search of that bubble of art which our grandfathers used to call Style.

R. T. C.

Unlocated.

The Rose-Leaf Romance.[3]

by R. T. CHANDLER.

It was one of those rare accomplished first novels which seem to find their publisher and their public as easily as love finds its young dream. It appeared under the auspices of a fine old firm, anonymously, though the fashion is out of date, and the world seized upon it at once. "A true rose-leaf romance, delicate as sea-spray in June, yet glittering and keen as diamond dust," wrote the wise, austere critics of the reviews who have read all books in all languages. "You simply *must* read it," said the feminine population to its friends, and even the great unpublished were not ashamed to be seen reading it. It created something less than a furore, perhaps, but far more than a succès d'estime. It was a book that politicians were compelled to glance at while dressing for dinner. Reviewers, to be in the mode, had to allude to it; it was a sound topic for breaking the ice at dinner parties; one gushed over it at tea, and took it out driving in Hyde Park. It was seen at country houses in canvas chairs on the lawn. Fathers of suburbia took it to their armchairs, scorning the newspaper. Retired majors seized on it gloweringly at the clubs, and stenographers devoured it over their infinitesimal lunches. In Paris it was conspicuous at Smith's bookshop in the Rue de Rivoli, and in America they demanded the life-history of the author, with photographs.

Somehow, apart from all this, I felt that it was an ideal of the first novel, that it must have been written in the way that first novels should be written, and I made bold to visit the author and ask him about it. He smiled in his genial way at my question.

"They have been written in strange and wonderful ways, these first novels," he said over his pipe; "in railway trains, by

77

the roadside, on tables in tea-shops, on the shores of South Sea islands, in the gun-rooms of Elizabethan manors, in the roof-gardens of skyscrapers, by windows overlooking the sea, and in back bedrooms of Bloomsbury that overlook nothing but a broken tool-shed. Still, I think that mine was written in as fine a setting as any.

"I lived at that time on a top floor of the Rue Tremaine, in the Hôtel Picanteur, not a hundred miles from Saint Sulpice. The Hôtel Picanteur is one of the shabbiest houses that ever were or ever could be. It is dull and dun-coloured, and receives a fine glare of the sun all day, yet seems to blink in this fine glare like some time-worn individual more familiar with the holes and corners than with the open parks of life, who has been suddenly dragged out of his hiding-place and set down in a room full of gay people. The Hôtel Picanteur has stood thus for sixty, eighty, perhaps more than a hundred years, without ever learning not to look taken aback by its situation. So, no doubt, it will stand until the end of time, eternally blinking, eternally dingy and dusty.

"Its interior, I may say, is not at all troubled by the sunlight. Its windows are perpetually unpolished, and shaded with faded red curtains. Its staircase is decrepit and ramshackle, its landings bare, and mantled in the deepest gloom. You can see strangers peering about on them at the yellow cards tacked to the doors, and looking all the time as if they fear some saturnine individual with anarchistic ethics may pop out of a dark doorway and acquaint their ribs relentlessly with a long stiletto. Strangers move there with ghostly tread and are eager to be gone. They descend the stairs with a cautious haste, and when they reach the street they look up at the musty façade with an air which says: 'Phew! I am lucky to get out of there without an injury.' Then they fly for the open boulevard and the friendly, agonising rattle of the steam trams. But the hour most portentous in the Hôtel Picanteur is the hour of dusk, when the heavy door shuts off the dying noises of the streets and the dark well of the staircase seems like a haunted tower. At that hour, too, the concierge has a habit of taking a late nap in the office on the left of the entrance, where he lies huddled and hidden in a deep chair behind the table and sends a long wailing snore out into the hall. I could never hear that snore without shuddering delightfully.

"I lived upon the barest and topmost landing, behind the most ramshackle door of all. My room, I confess, was a place of wonderful disorder. There were books everywhere—on the bed, on the floor—a row of them beside the grate, on the mantelpiece, and on all the chairs, where they left their outlines in dust when you took them up to sit down. There was a great deal of tobacco ash in my room, also. It was distinctly a bachelor apartment. In fact, the Hôtel Picanteur was distinctly a bachelor establishment; they were not faddy about cleanliness there.

"I lived so high up, not because I was poor, but because I liked to look out of my window over the roofs and see the grey buildings rioting noiselessly together in the august shadow of the church, I liked to hear the morning howl of the chairmender wafted up and attenuated by distance. I liked to poke my head out into the sun and see the blue-black-haired individuals in tight boots and diminutive bowler hats disputing at the café on the corner, so far down that their furious gestures reached me without any explanatory accompaniment of words. I liked to see the agent de police yawn serenely at the skies, or pull his sombre moustache with an air that seemed to meditate obscure villainies. I liked to see the bearded youths of eighteen in monstrous bow-ties go by with portfolios under their arms, hurling inaudible insult at each other. And at night I liked to lean out under the stars and add the secular incense of my pipe to the evening vapours of the city, while I mused about the general whimsicality of things. It was a wonderful location for a writer. One could look down on men from a proper altitude, and pity and laugh at them without impertinence. It was there that I, feeling myself aloof and viewing the world delicately, wrote my Rose-Leaf Romance, which is rather an aloof and delicate book."

It certainly is an aloof and delicate book, this prince of first novels. It has the fineness of a young mind in it, without any of the sentimentality of middle-age. It is the romance of charming gardens. The fragrance of roses blows across it always. It is based, as it must be, being patrician in tendency, upon a solid financial groundwork, but that is kept beautifully out of sight. The hero, Rafael Emmarca, dresses in cool flannels, and is wonderfully mannered; he has a quizzical way with him, and his talk is infinitely diverting. The heroine, Pauline Fontelle, is a feminine counterpart of the hero. She wears the most adorable costumes and moves with a sweet fresh gait; but she is a woman of the world and very far from a simpering ingénue. She uses a perfume with a vague elusive scent, not to be attributed definitely to any one flower, but compounding, as it were, the essences of all choice flowers, a perfume that hangs in the air of every scene where she is present and fastens bodilessly upon the senses. And her voice is as magical and elusive as the perfume she uses, such a voice as one might hear over water on a still night or from the shadows of suave trees in old-world gardens.

In the Rose-Leaf Romance everything is romantic and yet everything is wise. There is nothing mawkish about the book. Its characters are all witty and can, if occasion serve, be sarcastic to a degree. The story is slight in a way, but you do not deplore its slightness. There is the hero and the heroine, and that is the beautiful inevitable all—except for the fine delicate play of fine delicate emotions and thoughts and words, except for the moonlight and the sunlight and the roses, and the comfortable income which everybody has somewhere, decently out of the picture.

"These people used to walk with me when I went out," said the Author whimsically, "or sit with me in my somewhat unworthy room, or else meet me smiling in certain delightful spots of the city. There was Gaston Despiers, on the Cour-la-Reme, looking across the river at the Government offices. There was Georgine Stellenward in the Bois, and Rafael standing suavely on the steps of the Madeleine or strolling down the Rue de la Paix. I used to find Pauline at one of the tables outside the Café Riche, making pert, darting, flowery fun of the passers-by."

"This is all as it should be," said the visitor admiringly. "Now and again in the history of literature, that long record of grotesquely produced imaginings, it seems that a first novel is written as a first novel should be written. But what did you do when you found yourself growing famous?"

"I preserved my noble anonymity on the top-floor of the Hôtel Picanteur," he smiled. "I grew tolerably conceited over my namelessness. I would experience a vivid delight at the jeers of my friends of the Quartier.

" 'And all this three months' seclusion,' they used to say, 'What of it, hein?'

" 'You see I had a fire the other day,' I would answer, pointing to the grate.

"Then they would laugh. 'With the great souls it is always thus,' they would remark over innumerable cigarettes. 'For ten years they write and burn. After that one does something, perhaps.' "

I stood up to go, thanking the great man for his story. I found myself admiring his nervous, imaginative features, the ready fire of his eyes. Humbly I held out my hand, and he extended his at the same moment. But our hand-clasp was prevented, alas! by the hard, impassable, glossy surface of the mirror.

Still, I shall always consider the Rose-Leaf Romance, the high ideal of first novels, in substance, in setting, in style, and, not least, in the scene of its creation. It is a pity that it is still in the inkpot.

CHANDLER BEFORE MARLOWE

REVIEWS: 1911-1912

The Academy, 18 March 1911, pp. 328–29.

The Broad Highway.

BY JEFFERY FARNOL. (Sampson Low and Co. 6s.)

It is possible that Mr. Jeffery Farnol has not read "Lavengro," or that, having read it, he had yet no idea of making his present hero a recreation of George Borrow's romantic picture of himself. Yet Lavengro was an unusual person, not to be confounded with the common ruck of men, and it would be hard to believe that one who reflects many of his characteristic traits so closely as does Peter Vibart should have no connection with him. Firstly, as if to clinch the matter, Mr. Farnol has put his hero in the same epoch, amid similar scenes, and has made him what Lavengro was above all things—a wanderer. So good a reflection of Lavengro is Peter Vibart, indeed, that he possesses the same disabilities as that romantic but inestimable person. Mr. Farnol tries to fill him with a great love-passion, but the thing is impossible; the man who loves Charmian in the second part of "The Broad Highway" is not the Peter Vibart of the first half, but an ordinary moonstruck hero of sentimental romance, a creature of hothouse moods and unnatural speeches.

For the detailed account of his adventures we must refer the reader to the book itself, and he will be a person of very jaded appetite indeed who does not relish the freshness, the quietness, and the queer Borrow touch about Peter's encounter with the boastful pugilist, "Cragg by name and craggy by nature," and with the farmer who coveted his waistcoat, but with whom Peter refused to breakfast because his would-be host could not believe that that magnificent article of attire had cost 40s. in London. Then there was the affair of the insolent dandies, the duel in which Peter for the first time caught a distant glimpse of his cousin, the rescue of a damsel in distress from two offensive abductors, and her restoration to her lover, the meeting with the madman who was dogging Peter with murderous intent, and many other roadside happenings.

With the opening of the second part comes the entry of Charmian into the haunted cottage, on a night of storm, and pursued by Maurice Vibart. With him Peter does furious battle in the darkness, and at length sends him away unconscious in his own post-chaise. With these events, too, comes the degeneration of the story in manner though not, perhaps, in plot. The old solemn Borrow touch is gone, and with it the subtly humorous conversations and the atmosphere of pure romance. In their stead we have all the feverishness and over-rapidity of the second-rate sensational writer. The love passages of Charmian and Peter are forced and wearisome, and the doings of Black George, when maddened by jealousy, are told with that gloomy extravagance which suggests disordered nerves in the writer. Mr. Farnol regains something of his former quiet incisiveness in narrating Peter's escape from justice, when, the madman having at last found and killed his enemy, Peter suspects Charmian of the crime, and takes it upon himself; but the end, with its almost hysterical reconciliation of Peter and Charmian, who is, of course, the Lady Sophia Sefton of Cambourne, is but feeble stuff. It is impossible not to regret deeply the defects of the second half of Mr. Farnol's book, yet the first half is really very good. It is fine work of an uncommon order, and not merely a promise of future worth. We judge Mr. Farnol to be a young writer, and we do not at all regret his occasional crudeness, since it is merely undisciplined strength. But he must learn to avoid the feverish touch; that more than anything is death to true romance.

[Unsigned]

The Academy, 23 December 1911, pp. 796–97.

The Reason Why.

BY ELINOR GLYN. (Duckworth and Co. 6s.)

The frontispiece to Mrs. Glyn's latest novel is, in a way, a far better criticism of it than anything a hasty reviewer can write. It depicts a well-preserved lady of tall stature and voluptuous outlines throwing aside a fur cloak lined with amethyst silk in order to display a sort of bathing costume of sapphire blue, which appears to be her only garment. This article of attire reveals a quantity of white and rather pasty skin, an equally white and pasty face, with a ruby smear for a mouth, and two large, but not at all inscrutable, eyes. In the ears are pearl drops of such size as to be immediately set down as false, and the whole vision is surmounted by a badly-made wig of violent auburn hue.

Such is Zara, Countess Schulski, as seen by the powerful imagination of the enthusiastic illustrator. As a matter of fact, Zara is very beautiful and virtuous, and twenty-three years old, none of which truths one would gather from her portrait. She is driven, in order to provide for a delicate little brother, who is a musical prodigy, to enter upon a mercenary marriage with Tristram Lorrimer Guiscard Guiscard, twenty-fourth Baron Tancred, of Wrayth, in the county of Suffolk. She has been married already to some awful scoundrel of a foreigner, whose toy she was, and has consequently but a poor opinion of men. Owing to a misunderstanding of Tristram's (if we dare allude to a nobleman of such very ancient lineage by his Christian name) reasons for marrying her, which is the fault of her uncle, a millionaire with a house in Park-lane and a private lift, she treats Tristram coldly, and there is a scene after the wedding in which he swears she shall go down on her bended knees before he will speak words of love to her again. Gradually she falls in love with him, but she is pale as death all the while. Aristocratic society flutters in admiration about her, remarking upon her troubled looks. Tristram becomes wilder and wilder, loses all taste for his food, suspects her of infidelity, and departs for the Soudan. But the financier, meantime reformed by the softer passion, allows Zara to explain matters which she promised to conceal, and she reaches Tristram's rooms in London just in time to fall into his arms and murmur, "Tu sais que je t'aime."

Mrs. Glyn writes with an enormous amount of sensuous zest, which suggests that she really believes her work to be worth doing. It is this quality that lifts her out of the sea of bad fiction to a position of some notoriety, but to the critical reader it only condemns her, in the literary sense, the more securely.

[Unsigned]

The Academy, 22 June 1912, pp. 774–75.

The Art of Loving and Dying

The Drama of Love and Death:
A Study of Human Evolution and Transfiguration.
BY EDWARD CARPENTER. (George Allen and Co. 5s. net.)

What was the beginning of love, and what part does it play in the destinies of life? What rôle worthy of its power over the minds and bodies of men can we assign to it? How shall we explain its survival long after its task of reproduction is done, and the fact that its force and rarity are greatest when that task is least regarded? Why does it triumph over death so completely that at times it appears to devote itself deliberately to death, as if death were a necessary incident in its career?

Does the soul survive after death, and if so what is the soul which survives—the small personal self which we know and weary of, or some deeper self to which we are all but strangers? Are there in the beginnings of the race any indications of a soul existing before birth—indications which may clearly point to its continuance after death? What are the psychical phenomena of death? What form does the liberated spirit take, what is its pilgrimage and what its goal? And if its journeys and its deeds are wonderful beyond the dreams of man, what purpose is served by its confinement in the flesh?

Such are the questions which Mr. Carpenter asks and answers in his new book. Beginning with the Protozoa, called "immortal" because they do not die bodily but divide and redivide to produce an almost infinite succession of new creatures, he traces the beginnings of love from its first task of reviving two worn-out individuals by fusion of their forces. He points out with what strange cunning the most elementary forms of life perform these processes, and goes on to speak of human love, dwelling particularly upon its spiritual effect and its rejuvenating powers. He insists, as it is now the fashion to insist, upon an Art of Love, on the fact that there is a right and a wrong way of loving, quite apart from morality, and that the knowledge of the right way is criminally neglected in the teaching of youth.

If there is an Art of Love, there is also an Art of Dying. The full evils of a death which is artificially made revolting cannot be realised until one begins to calculate what takes place immediately after death, and how far the circumstances of its parting influence the liberated soul. Such speculations are bound to become fanciful, and are liable to be sneered at on that account, but we feel that we have no right to smile overmuch when Mr. Carpenter proceeds to divide the Self into four parts and to explain what happens to each of them. First there is the eternal and immortal soul or self, which remains much the same after death as before it—possibly as before birth. Second is the "inner personal ego or human soul, that which we know of a man on his highest plane, his affections, his courage, his wit, his love of beauty and all his finer attributes." The destiny of this self is the most obscure and varied of the four; to its account, according to our author, are to be laid, both in life and afterwards, such things as forewarnings, telepathic messages and spiritual phenomena. This self wanders on the borderland of life, and the continuity and scope of its after existence may be determined largely by its powers and development on earth. Third comes the "outer personal or animal self," which dies normally as completely as the fourth self, the actual body.

This theory has the advantage of explaining many things which are obscure, but it has the disadvantage, particularly as regards the second and third divisions of itself, of depending for a great deal of its force upon a ready acceptance of clairvoyance, ghosts, and spiritualistic phenomena of various kinds. Mr. Carpenter declares his mind to be open on this subject, but he gives a great deal of space to describing various spiritual appearances and records, and they certainly flavour the last half of the book strongly.

Of a like uncertainty seems the theory, cited here with approbation, that the personal soul consists of a framework of "centresomes" or active centres of the cells, which, owing to their minuteness, can pass through the tissues at death and, keeping their distances like soldiers on parade, give the appearance of a ghost body, when they become visible, as apparently they do on occasion. The idea is wonderfully ingenious, but is it not a little trivial?

When the author treats of reincarnation, and of the purpose of the soul's incarnation, he seems to walk on surer and loftier ground. The possibility of the individual character of a man having been once clothed just as it is in a former body, and of its being destined to be thus clothed again in the future, he demolishes utterly by showing how entirely the perceptible individuality of a man—by which alone we know him—is a product of the circumstances of his life, his parents, his places of abode, his friends, his habits, his activities. The reincarnation of a deeper and less characteristic self is not to be denied so easily. Only by some such method, we are told, can the racial self such as we see in animals pass by way of the more distinct but still not quite individual self of civilised man on and on until it becomes a pure and perfect creation which can nevermore be mingled and confounded with the "all-soul" of the universe. The confinement of the flesh produces the perfection of personality, which is the aim of life, and which, without that imprisonment, would have remained but a vague flux and reflux of obscure forces. But the war of life, the struggle in these narrow surroundings, is bitter, and after death for a time at least comes sleep.

When one thinks of the strange contradictions of our mortal life, the hopelessly antagonistic elements, the warring of passions, the shattering of ideals, the stupor of monotony: the soul like a bird shut in a cage or with bright wings draggled in the mire; the horrible sense of sin which torments some people, the mad impulses which tyrannise over others; the alterations of one's own personality on different days, or at different depths and planes of consciousness; the supraliminal and the subliminal; the smug Upper-self, with its petty satisfactions and its precise and precious logic, and the great Under-self now rising (in the hour of death) like some vast shadowy figure or genius, out of the abyss of being—when one thinks of all this one feels that if there is to be any sanity or sequence in the conclusion, it must mean a long period of brooding and reconciliation, and even of sleep.

After a time the soul arises, a giant refreshed, and sets about its work, either once more on earth, or in more ethereal places. But what that work is and wherein it lies a charm so great that the happiest man dreaming of it may turn his face to the wall contentedly, are points which are not here elucidated. For the inadequacy of the delights of heaven, once heaven ceases to be regarded as a perfected material earth, is a thing which has paralysed all the philosophies.

We have sketched some of the lines of thought in this volume at a considerable length because they exhibit not only a very original plan and many unusual arguments, but also a sincere attempt to reconcile the theories of science with the modern mystical attitude. Fifty years ago, as Mr. Carpenter points out, science was thought to have explained away all grounds of belief; people talked about dead worlds and a mechanical universe. Now science has proceeded to the opposite extreme. So little is the universe beyond our ken an empty void that our bodies seem rather a veil betwixt our confined life and a far richer and more various existence behind. So little is life regarded now as a mere mechanism that the minutest cells are said to be sentient, creative and self-willed beings, with pains and pleasures and purposes of their own. Upon this scientific view Mr. Carpenter has raised the speculative structure of his book. Yet after all, greatly as the newer dreams transcend the old Victorian scientists' gloomy prognostications, are they not a substitution of a very complicated for a comparatively simple mechanism of life? Is not the difference largely one of detail, and is not the new idea of the after-life with its transcendental rhapsodies about the great deeds of the liberated soul and the picture of a heaven like a laboratory in which the chemicals make endless experiments upon each other—is not this prospect almost as unsatisfying to the mind as that of peaceful annihilation? In the end we are driven to take all these theories, however exact and scientific, as figuratively as we take the poet's dream; for to take them in sober earnest both the imagination and the sense of humour refuse point blank. Nevertheless, if Mr. Carpenter has not given us a creed (and we are perhaps too ready nowadays to look for a creed in every theorising volume), he has given us a brilliant and original book, which reveals the best of the typical qualities of our age.

[Unsigned]

The Academy, 22 June 1912, pp. 776–77.

The Rural Labourer at Home

Change in the Village.
BY GEORGE BOURNE. (Duckworth and Co. 5s. net.)

The task of tracing the change of the village peasant into the
modern labouring man, the accompanying alterations in his
surroundings, the narrowing of his mind in one direction and
its widening in another, together with a reckoning up of the
faults of the present and the hopes for the future, Mr. George
Bourne has here accomplished with thoroughness, patience,
good nature, and a gentle, but determined, insistence of un-
palatable facts. To say that his book is very interesting when it
deals with a subject which must on the surface be unattractive
to many people, when the village chosen for the type is without
a touch of romance either in history or situation, and its people
are set down before us with all the commonplace sordidness
which a casual unimaginative mind might see in them, that
alone is high praise.

The labouring man is a familiar figure in our civilisation.
Most people are aware that he has a habit of smoking shag, that
he sees virtues in the public-house which are not apparent to
the cultivated mind, that he walks in an ungainly fashion, car-
ries his lunch in a red handkerchief, often goes unshaven from
week-end to week-end, and usually lives in a small, dingy cottage, in the rear of which washing can be seen hung out on
several days of the week. A few may know beyond this that he
does most of the unpleasant work of the world for very small
pay, that his manners towards strangers, particularly of his own
class, are often a good deal better, taking them all in all, than
those of the middle classes who employ him, that he is a very
expert gardener, and that the animosity which he is supposed
to feel towards men of property is, as a rule, a myth. All this and
very much more Mr. Bourne tells us, chatting in a genial way,

and showing himself so little a partisan that he leaves us ignorant of his political views. He takes us into the labouring man's
home, shows us in what constrained spaces his family have to
live, and how little an exalted ideal of cleanliness is possible
there. He shows us the silent heroism of a body of men who
can afford to think no toil too exacting or unpleasant, who can
never throughout their lives honestly put the pleasure of the
moment before the possibility of earning a shilling. Mr. Bourne
is not a pessimist, and yet the picture he paints is very drab. It
would be hard to imagine anyone wanting to be a modern labourer, and when we have said that we have made a final criticism upon the existence of the labouring class. Life for them
involves so many unbreakable rules, orders them to do so many
unpleasant things, gives them so little choice as to the time and
manner of doing them, and denies them so many pleasures
which others deem necessities, that their good humour and
energy are among the most powerful arguments to be found for
the future greatness of humanity.

Many of the discomforts of the labourer's present position
Mr. Bourne attributes to the enclosure of the commons, but it
is not to be inferred from this that he indulges in anything like
denunciation of property owners. His quarrel, on the whole, is
not with the land-owning class, but with the commercial ideal,
its overdriven "thrift," its thoughtless use of superfluous ma-
chinery to make a hundred unnecessary bad articles where one
necessary good thing would have sufficed. Such an indictment
belongs rather to philosophy than to practical politics, but the
effect of commercial methods upon the labouring man is a
ludicrous comment on the current economic. The precise result is that he, with the smallest wages in the community, buys
everything at the highest price, because he can buy so little at
a time, and because, when there is question of any large outlay,
he is driven beyond possibility of practical wisdom to buy what
is cheap and rotten.

Into the details of this book it is not necessary for a review to
enter. We have shown its spirit, and its scope is sufficiently in-
dicated by such chapter headings as: Man and Wife, Drink,

Ways and Means, The Peasant System, Competition, Humiliation, The Want of Book-Learning, Emotional Starvation, The Children's Need, etc. Of plans for the future Mr. Bourne gives us little; he is modest, and declares himself a friendly, unskilled, unstatistical observer. He aims at showing just what the labouring man is, and with what he has to contend, and he succeeds perfectly.

[Unsigned]

CHANDLER AFTER MARLOWE

1955-1958

Sold to the *Atlantic Monthly* but not published.

Requiem[4]

There is a moment after death when the face is beautiful,
When the soft, tired eyes are closed and the pain is over,
And the long, long innocence of love comes gently in
For a moment more, in quiet to hover.

There is a moment after death, yet hardly a moment,
When the bright clothes hang in the scented closet
And the lost dream fades and slowly fades,
When the silver bottles and the glass, and the empty mirror,
And three long hairs in a brush and a folded kerchief,
And the fresh made bed and the fresh, plump pillows
On which no head will lie
Are all that is left of the long wild dream.

But there are always the letters.

I hold them in my hand, tied with green ribbon
Neatly and firmly by the soft, strong fingers of love.
The letters will not die.
They will wait and wait for the stranger to come and read them.
He will come slowly out of the mists of time and change,
He will come slowly, diffidently, down the years,
He will cut the ribbon and spread the letters apart,
And carefully, carefully read them page by page.

And the long long innocence of love will come softly in
Like a butterfly through an open window in summer,
For a moment more in quiet to hover.
But the stranger will never know.
The stranger will be I.

RAYMOND CHANDLER
        Jan. 16th 1955

Sonnet 13

What man designed a Doric architrave
For some late-learned ~~erotic~~ *critic* to ~~declare~~ *proclaim* :
~~Or~~ serve the clean, hard ~~living~~ *line to* some people rave
~~Or~~ tortured painting in a tortured frame.

The Greeks new better, purity was their aim:
"Das Ding an Sich", ~~but~~ always lay the grave *or AUGHT*
In waiting, and the silence and the ~~maggot,~~ *night*
This was (at last) the honour which they bought.

Man is too often nobler than his fate.

If God is near, is it so small a thing
That men long dead such beauty could create,
That sweet birds sing, grass grows, and lovers mate ?
Have we ~~high~~ *deep* senses, ~~deep~~ hearts, and wondering eyes
Merely to wait, till some ~~lost~~ poet dies ?

Raymond Chandler,

Spring, 1958.

WORKING DRAFT. Special Collections, University of California, Los Angeles, Library. First published in *Tutto Marlowe Investigatore*, I (Mondadori, 1970).

100

Sonnet 13

What man designed a Doric architrave
For some late-learned critic to proclaim:
"They servedthe clean, hard line. Some people rave
"Of tortured painting in a tortured frame.
"The Greeks knew better, purity was their aim:
"'Das Ding an Sich'." But always lay the grave
In waiting, and the silence and the naught.
This was the honour which at last they bought.
Man is too often nobler than his fate.
If God is near, is it so small a thing
That man long dead such beauty could create,
That sweet birds sing, grass grows, and lovers mate ?
Have we deep senses, hearts, and wondering eyes
Merely to wait until some poet dies ?

Raymond Chandler
Spring -   1958.

FINAL TYPESCRIPT. Special Collections, University of California, Los Angeles, Library. Previously unpublished.

NOTES

Endnotes

Note for "The Unknown Love"

1. In *Twentieth Century Authors First Supplement*, edited by Stanley J. Kunitz (New York: Wilson, 1955), Chandler states: "My first poem was composed at the age of nineteen, on a Sunday, in the bathroom, and was published in *Chambers' Journal*. I am fortunate in not possessing a copy, but I can remember some of it and I think it would go over well if recited by Margaret O'Brien. I had, to be frank, the qualifications to become a pretty good second-rate poet, but that means nothing because I have the type of mind that can become a pretty good second-rate anything, and without much effort. I used to do mostly paragraphs (which I lifted from foreign language papers) for the *Westminster Gazette* and verses and sketches."

Note for "Organ Music"

2. Unlocated—I have seen this poem only in a proof.

Note for "The Rose-Leaf Romance"

3. Unlocated—I have seen this sketch only as a mounted clipping.

Note for "Requiem"

4. Chandler's wife, Cissy, died 12 December 1954.

Textual Notes

N.B. The poems were originally set in roman type; they have been set in oblique in the present volume.

"The Soul's Defiance"

    line 8   Into   [into

"The Reformer"

    line 52   *a broken 'f' in 'foul' produced the nonsense word 'joul'*

"The Genteel Artist"

56.26   work,   [work.

"The Tropical Romance"

69.10   hack₄   [hack.

"The Rose-Leaf Romance"

81.7   Quartier."   [Quartier.
81.9   hein?' "   [hein?'

Review of *The Broad Highway*

85.14   A   [The

Review of *Change in the Village*

94.19   handerchief   [handkerchief

Chandler Checklist

This checklist includes books by Chandler and all of his stories and articles from 1933. It does not list books reprinted under changed titles, reviews, or published letters. The material in Chandler Before Marlowe *has also been omitted.*

BOOKS

The Big Sleep. New York: Knopf, 1939. London: Hamish Hamilton, 1939.

Farewell, My Lovely. New York and London: Knopf, 1940. London: Hamish Hamilton, 1940.

The High Window. New York: Knopf, 1942. London: Hamish Hamilton, 1943.

The Lady in the Lake. New York: Knopf, 1943. London: Hamish Hamilton, 1944.

Five Murderers. New York: Avon, 1944. Contents: "Goldfish," "Spanish Blood," "Blackmailers Don't Shoot," "Guns at Cyrano's," "Nevada Gas."

Five Sinister Characters. New York: Avon, 1945. Contents: "Trouble Is My Business," "Pearls Are a Nusiance," "I'll Be Waiting." "The King in Yellow," "Red Wind."

Finger Man. New York: Avon, 1946. Contents: "Finger Man," "The Bronze Door," "Smart-Aleck Kill," "The Simple Art of Murder."

The Little Sister. London: Hamish Hamilton, 1949. Boston: Houghton Mifflin, 1949.

The Simple Art of Murder. Boston: Houghton, 1950. London: Hamish Hamilton, 1950. Reprints twelve stories and "The Simple Art of Murder."

The Long Good-Bye. London: Hamish Hamilton, 1953. Boston: Houghton Mifflin, 1954.

Playback. London: Hamish Hamilton, 1958. Boston: Houghton Mifflin, 1958.

Raymond Chandler Speaking, ed. Dorothy Gardiner and Kathrine Sorley Walker. London: Hamish Hamilton, 1962. Boston: Houghton Mifflin, 1962.

Killer in the Rain, introduction by Philip Durham. London: Hamish Hamilton, 1964. Boston: Houghton Mifflin, 1964. Contents: "Killer in the Rain," "The Curtain," "Try the Girl," "Mandarin's Jade," "Bay City Blues," "The Lady in the Lake."

Chandler Before Marlowe, ed. Matthew J. Bruccoli, foreword by Jacques Barzun. Columbia: University of South Carolina Press, 1973. Limited printing.

PERIODICAL APPEARANCES

STORIES

"Blackmailers Don't Shoot," *Black Mask* (December 1933).

"Smart Aleck Kill," *Black Mask* (July 1934).

"Finger Man," *Black Mask* (October 1934).

"Killer in the Rain," *Black Mask* (January 1935).

"Nevada Gas," *Black Mask* (June 1935).

"Spanish Blood," *Black Mask* (November 1935).

"Guns at Cyrano's," *Black Mask* (January 1936).

"The Man Who Liked Dogs," *Black Mask* (March 1936).

"Noon Street Nemesis," *Detective Fiction Weekly* (30 May 1936)— later titled "Pick-up on Noon Street."

"Goldfish," *Black Mask* (June 1936).

"The Curtain," *Black Mask* (September 1936).

"Try the Girl," *Black Mask* (January 1937).

"Mandarin's Jade," *Dime Detective* (November 1937).

"Red Wind," *Dime Detective* (January 1938).

"The King in Yellow," *Dime Detective* (March 1938).

"Bay City Blues," *Dime Detective* (June 1938).

"The Lady in the Lake," *Dime Detective* (January 1939).

"Pearls Are a Nuisance," *Dime Detective* (April 1939).

"Trouble Is My Business," *Dime Detective* (August 1939).

"I'll Be Waiting," *Saturday Evening Post* (14 October 1939).

"The Bronze Door," *Unknown* (November 1939).

"No Crime in the Mountains," *Detective Story* (September 1941).

"Professor Bingo's Snuff," *Park East* (June–August 1951); *Go* (June–July 1951).

"Marlowe Takes on the Syndicate," *London Daily Mail* (6–10 April 1959). Reprinted as "Wrong Pigeon," "Philip Marlowe's Last Case," and "The Pencil."

ARTICLES

"The Simple Art of Murder," *Atlantic Monthly* (December 1944). There are two different articles with this title—see below.

"Writers in Hollywood," *Atlantic Monthly* (November 1945).

"The Hollywood Bowl," *Atlantic Monthly* (January 1947).

"Oscar Night in Hollywood," *Atlantic Monthly* (March 1948).

"Ten Greatest Crimes of the Century," *Cosmopolitan* (October 1948).

"The Simple Art of Murder," *Saturday Review of Literature* (15 April 1950).

"Ten Percent of Your Life," *Atlantic Monthly* (February 1952).

"The Detective Story as an Art Form," *Crime Writer* (Spring 1959).

ABOUT CHANDLER

Philip Durham, *Down These Mean Streets A Man Must Go.* Chapel Hill: University of North Carolina Press, 1963.

Matthew J. Bruccoli, *Raymond Chandler: A Checklist.* Kent, Ohio: Kent State University Press, 1968.

,

Chandler Before Marlowe

Composed in Linotype Electra of the 11-point size set on 13-point slugs by Heritage Printers, Inc. with selected lines of display in Goudy Old Style and Ultra Bodoni. Printed offset by Universal Lithographers, Inc. on Warren's University Text, an acid-free paper noted for its longevity. The paper was expressly watermarked for the University of South Carolina Press with the Press colophon. Binding by L. H. Jenkins, Inc. in Scott Graphics' Kivar 5 over .088 boards. Designed by Robert L. Nance.